The Foundry was Methodism's First Meeting Place in London

THE ESSENTIALS
OF
METHODISM

by

Rev. Dr. James T. Reuteler, Ph.D.
Covenant Bible Studies
Aurora, Colorado
2013

1

Lovely Lane Chapel in Baltimore on Christmas of 1784

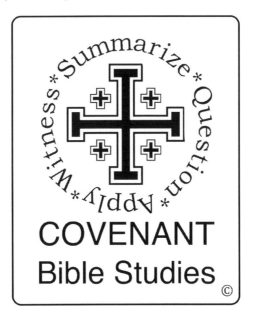

Rev. Dr. James T. Reuteler, Ph.D.
Covenant Bible Studies
3692 South Quatar Way
Aurora, Colorado 80018
Jim@Reuteler.org
720-320-7675

TABLE OF CONTENTS

INTRODUCTION

The essentials of Methodism are original sin, justification by faith, and holiness of heart and life.

John Wesley

Essentials

Every Methodist should know Methodism's rich past, but even more than that, every Methodist should be familiar with the essentials that leads us into to a deep relationship with God and with one another. This is a book about both the past, the present, and the future. If we don't know where we came from, it will be difficult to know where we are going.

This book is for those Methodists who don't think we have a theology, and that they are free to pick and choose whatever attracts them. I shall use Methodism's basic documents, such as *The General Rules*, the *Methodist Articles of Religion* and the *Evangelical United Brethren's Confession of Faith*.

While I haven't been given any authority to merge these historical documents, I have taken the Liberty to do so. This wasn't difficult to do. Most of them merged together quite nicely, except for the paragraph on Sanctification. The *Evangelical United Brethren's Confession of Faith* included Sanctification. The *Methodist Articles of Religion* did not. This does not mea that there's a disagreement over Sanctification. There is not. Sanctification has always been a part of Methodist theology.

Like the *Articles of Religion*, the *General Rules* have been frozen in time. That's good in one sense. It keeps us from straying too far from our roots, but it also keeps us from revising them to be relevant for our own time. The only people asked if they know the *General Rules* are ministerial candidates seeking ordination. They are also asked if they will keep them.

So, instead of carrying a small card with the *Generals Rules* on it to help us to walk faithfully as disciples of Christ, we now have the *Social Principles*, which hardly anyone reads, except when there's a disagreement. Since there are several disagreements on social issues, I chose to include those social issues which are most controversial.

In addition to naming the essentials of Methodism, John Wesley also called the Class Meeting the "sinew (muscle) of Methodism." The Class Meeting has almost disappeared from Methodism, but it has returned with the New General Rule of Discipleship. As the Class Meeting met to watch over one another in love, Covenant Discipleship Groups meet to do the same with an updated General Rule.[1]

This is a different kind of book. One might call it a study book. In another sense, it's a reference book. I have taught these ten lessons to new as well as longtime Methodists. When we join a United Methodist Church, we make the following covenant:

1. To renounce the spiritual forces of wickedness, reject the evil powers of the world, and repent of their sin;

2. To accept the freedom and power God gives them to resist evil, injustice, and oppression;

3. To confess Jesus Christ as Savior, put their whole trust in his grace, and promise to serve him as their Lord;

4. To remain faithful members of Christ's holy church and serve as Christ's representatives in the world;

5. To be loyal to Christ through The United Methodist Church and do all in their power to strengthen its ministries;

6. To faithfully participate in its ministries by their prayers, their presence, their gifts, their service, and their witness;

7. To receive and profess the Christian faith as contained in the Scriptures of the Old and New Testaments.

These are serious questions. They don't call for some voluntary association of people who believe whatever they want. They call us into a covenant community. These are the things that make up the essentials of our faith community.

Rev. Dr. James T. Reuteler, Ph.D.

---

[1] See David Watson's book, *Covenant Discipleship* (Nashville, Discipleship Resources), 1991.

1. METHODISM

The Story of Methodism
by Rupert E. Davies

A Brief Biography of John Wesley

Quotes from John Wesley

THE STORY OF METHODISM

Origins

John Wesley, the founder of Methodism, was born in 1703. After ordination in the Church of England, he was elected a Fellow of Lincoln College at Oxford in 1726. In the following year he left Oxford temporarily to act as curate to his father, the rector of Epworth. Back in Oxford, to which his younger brother Charles had now come, he found himself a member and soon the leader of a group of earnest students pledged to frequent attendance at Holy Communion, serious study of the Bible, and regular visitation of the filthy Oxford prisons. The members of this group received the sobriquet of Methodists.

In 1735 both John and Charles Wesley set out for Georgia to be pastors to the colonists and missionaries (it was hoped) to the Indians, at the invitation of the founder of the colony, James Edward Oglethorpe. They were unsuccessful in their pastoral work and did no missionary work. The brothers returned to England conscious of their lack of genuine Christian faith. They looked for help from members of the Church of the Brethren, who were staying in England for a while before joining Moravian settlements in the American colonies; among these Peter Böhler was especially important. On May 24, 1738, John Wesley's Journal narrates that he "felt" his "heart strangely warmed" and continues, "I felt I did trust in Christ, Christ alone, for salvation; and an assurance was given me that He had taken away my sins, even mine, and saved me from the law of sin and death." Charles Wesley had reported a similar experience a few days previously.

Some months later John Wesley was invited by his friend George Whitefield, also an Anglican clergyman who had undergone a "conversion experience," to come to the city of Bristol and help to preach to the colliers of Kingswood Chase, just outside the city, where human conditions were at their lowest. Wesley came and found himself, much against his will, preaching in the open air. This enterprise was the beginning of the Methodist Revival. Whitefield and Wesley at first worked together but later separated on doctrinal grounds: Whitefield believed in double predestination; Wesley regarded this as an erroneous doctrine and insisted that the love of God was universal.

Under the leadership at first of Whitefield and afterward of Wesley the movement rapidly gained ground among those who felt themselves neglected by the Church of England. Wesley differed from contemporary Anglicans not in doctrines but in emphases: he claimed to have reinstated

11

the biblical doctrines that a man may be assured of his salvation and that, by the power of the Holy Spirit, he is capable of attaining perfect love for God and his fellows in this life. Wesley's helpers included only a few ordained clergymen and notably his brother Charles, who wrote more than 6,000 hymns to express the message of the Revival. In spite of Wesley's wish that the Methodist Society would never leave the Church of England, relations with Anglicans were often strained.

In 1784, when there was a shortage of ordained ministers in America after the Revolution, the Bishop of London refused to ordain a Methodist for the United States. Wesley, acting in an emergency and on biblical principles that allow (as he thought) a presbyter to ordain, ordained Thomas Coke as superintendent and two others as presbyters. In the same year, by a Deed of Declaration, he appointed a Conference of 100 men to govern the Society of Methodists after his death.

The definite break with the Church of England came in 1795, four years after Wesley's death. After this, English Methodism, with vigorous outposts in Ireland, Scotland, and Wales, rapidly developed as a church. But in order not to perpetuate the split from the Church of England, it was reluctant at first to ordain with the laying on of hands. Its system centered in the annual Conference (at first of ministers only, later thrown open to laypeople), which controlled all its affairs. The country was divided into districts and the districts into circuits, or groups of congregations. The ministers were appointed to the circuits, and each circuit was led by a superintendent, though much power remained in the hands of the local trustees.

This tightly knit system enabled the Wesleyan Methodist Church to grow rapidly throughout the 19th century, at the end of which it counted 450,000 members. The growth was largest in the expanding industrial areas. There their faith enabled Methodist workers, men and women, to endure economic hardship, while at the same time working for the alleviation of poverty. Because their faith encouraged them to live simply, their economic status tended to rise, with the unintended result that Wesleyan Methodism became a middle-class church that was not immune to the excessive stress on the individual in material and spiritual matters that marked the Victorian age.

At the same time the autocratic habits of some ministers in authority, notably Jabez Bunting, an outstanding but sometimes ruthless leader, alienated many of the more ardent and democratic spirits, and there was a series of schisms. The Methodist New Connexion broke off in 1797, the Primitive Methodists in 1811, the Bible Christians in 1815, and the United Methodist Free Churches in 1857.

The smaller Methodist groups were in closer contact with the working classes than the Wesleyans and provided the leadership in early trade unionism to an extent disproportionate to their size. The Wesleyans were at first conservative in politics but in the second half of the 19th century identified themselves more and more with the liberalism of William Gladstone.

A movement to reunite the Methodist groups began about the turn of the century and reached success in two stages. In 1907 the Methodist New Connexion, the Bible Christians, and the United Methodist Free Churches joined to form the United Methodist Church; and in 1932 the Wesleyan Methodist Church, the Primitive Methodist Church, and the United Methodist Church came together to form the Methodist Church.

The Methodist Church has shared with the other English churches in the numerical decline that began about 1910. This decline, together with changes in modern life and thought, roused it out of its Victorian complacency and filled it with a desire to express Wesley's original ideals in a contemporary form. It continued to plan new attempts at evangelism. Its concern for education, shown especially in the development of Kingswood School (Wesley's foundation) and other boarding schools, as well as in the training of Christian teachers at Westminster and Southlands colleges, has not abated. Its strong social interest has expanded from preoccupation with total abstinence to a wide range of national and international issues, especially those connected with race, poverty, and peace.

The Methodist Church involved itself in the ecumenical movement when it began in 1910. Thereafter the church shared in all negotiations for church union. Relations with the Church of England improved so much by the 1960s that a plan for the reunion of the two churches (in two stages) was approved in principle by both in 1965. The final form of the plan was approved by the Methodist Church with a very large majority in 1969, but the Church of England did not muster a large enough majority to bring the plan into effect. The same thing happened in 1972.

Proposals for a "Covenant for Visible Unity," to include the United Reformed Church and the Moravian Church as well as the Methodists and the Anglicans, were put to the churches in 1982; once again the Anglican vote fell short, while the other churches were in favour. Most Methodists were grievously disappointed, but many threw themselves into projects in their own neighborhood intended to realize locally the unity that was not possible nationally. In these projects Anglicans, United Reformed Church people, and sometimes Baptists and Roman Catholics, are taking part.

As a founder member of the British Council of Churches and the World Council of Churches, the Methodist Church has shared fully in the activities of these councils and provided many leaders. Official discussion with Roman Catholics on national and world levels has revealed a surprising degree of agreement while promoting tolerance and understanding of previously contentious issues.

The first woman was ordained to "The Ministry of Word and Sacraments" in 1974. This was the climax of many years of discussion and controversy. It indicated a growing appreciation of the place of women in the life of the church. The theological objections had been carefully considered and rejected before the final step was taken.

Methodism in America

Methodism was taken to America by immigrants from Ireland who had been converted by John Wesley. Wesley also sent preachers, and by far the most successful of these was Francis Asbury, a blacksmith, who arrived in 1771 and covered vast distances. He adapted Wesley's principles to the needs both of the settled communities and of the frontier. Wesley took the side of the English government at the time of the Revolution, but Asbury aligned himself with the new American republic. Wesley sent the men whom he had ordained as presbyters, with Thomas Coke as superintendent, to help Asbury. The Methodist Episcopal Church was constituted in 1784 and regarded itself as autonomous. Asbury and Coke allowed themselves to be called bishops.

The next 50 years saw a remarkable advance led by the circuit riders who preached to the frontiersmen in simple terms. The slavery issue split the Methodist Church into two: the Methodist Episcopal Church and the Methodist Episcopal Church, South (organized in 1845). After the Civil War both churches increased rapidly and became gradually assimilated to the general pattern of American Protestantism. When it was clear that the old issues no longer divided them, they began to move together. But it was not until 1939 that they came together to form The Methodist Church. The Methodist Protestant Church, a smaller group, joined in the same union.

The church in the South lost its black members before and during the Civil War. At the time of the union the Central Jurisdiction was formed for all the black members wherever they lived; it existed alongside the other jurisdictions that were determined by geography. The Central Jurisdiction was abolished in 1968; and black Methodists are now integrated in the church.

The originally German-speaking Evangelical United Brethren Church, itself a union of the Church of the United Brethren in Christ and the

Evangelical Church, was united with The Methodist Church in 1968 to form the United Methodist Church. Women were given limited clergy rights in 1924 and were accepted for full ordination in 1956.

Methodist Teachings

Methodism is marked by an acceptance of the doctrines of historic Christianity; by an emphasis on those doctrines that indicate the power of the Holy Spirit to confirm the faith of the believer and transform his personal life; by insistence that the heart of religion lies in personal relationship with God; by simplicity of worship; by the partnership of ordained ministers and laity in the worship and administration of the church; by a concern for the underprivileged and the betterment of social conditions; and (at least in its British form) by the formation of small groups for mutual encouragement and edification.

All Methodist churches profess allegiance to the Scriptures as the supreme guide to faith and practice. They welcome the findings of modern biblical scholarship (except for the fundamentalist groups to be found within them). They accept the historic creeds and hold themselves to be in the tradition of the Protestant Reformation. Arguments about the virgin birth and the physical resurrection of Jesus do not greatly concern Methodists; they allow for differences of conviction on these points within the historic faith. They emphasize the teaching about Christian perfection, interpreted as "perfect love," which is associated with John Wesley, who held that every Christian should aspire to this by the help of the Holy Spirit.

Methodist churches assert the value of infant baptism and the need to receive regularly the sacrament of the Lord's Supper, in which they believe Christ to be truly present, though they have no precise definition of the manner of his presence. They believe themselves to be integral parts of the one, holy, catholic, and apostolic church, and the ministers to be true ministers of Word and sacrament in the church of God.

Worship and Organization

Patterns of service

Methodist worship everywhere is partly liturgical, partly spontaneous. John Wesley regularly used the Anglican Book of Common Prayer and adapted it for use in the United States. He also conducted services that included extemporaneous prayer. His custom was continued in Britain. In the 20th century Anglican Morning Prayer gradually dropped out of Methodism, but Anglican Holy Communion continued until the Liturgical Movement impelled all churches, Roman Catholic and Protestant alike, to revise their liturgies. The Methodist Service Book (1975), written in a modern language, offers much opportunity for congregational participation. The Sunday Service, or Holy Communion, restores the traditional fourfold pattern—the offering of bread and wine, the thanksgiving, the breaking of the bread, and the sharing of the elements. Non-liturgical services, which constitute the majority, tend to be stereotyped although they claim to be spontaneous. Far more services are conducted by lay preachers than by ordained ministers.

In American Methodism services are rarely conducted by laypeople. The Liturgical Movement affected the Book of Worship (1965), the Ordinal (1980), and the United Methodist Hymnal, subtitled The Book of United Methodist Worship (1988), which is arranged to eliminate all traces of sexism.

Hymns are important in all branches of Methodism. Those of Charles Wesley are still dominant in British Methodism, but they are mingled with many contemporary hymns as well as hymns from other traditions. In Hymns and Psalms (1983) certain changes were made in order to eliminate sexist overtones. American books contain fewer hymns by Wesley.

Polity

In the churches of the British tradition the annual Conference is the supreme authority for doctrine, order, and practice. All ministers have parity of status, but special functions are exercised by the president and secretary of the Conference, the chairmen of districts, the secretaries of divisions, and superintendents. District affairs are regulated by Synods, Circuits by Circuit Meetings, local Societies by Church Councils. The American tradition is episcopal; the bishops are elected by the Jurisdictional Conferences, which, like the General Conference, meet every four years. Each diocese has an annual Conference and is divided into District Conferences, each with its superintendent. The dioceses are combined into five Jurisdictions that cover the nation. The circuit system is not developed. A minister is ordained first deacon, then elder.

In the United States the African Methodist Episcopal Zion Church and the African Methodist Episcopal Church antedate the explosion of the slavery question; the Colored(now "Christian") Methodist Episcopal Church was founded as a result of it. All three are exclusively black but follow the doctrine and organization of the United Methodist Church.

There are minority Methodist churches in most European countries. Those in Italy and Portugal are of English origin, that in Germany is of mixed English and American origin; the rest are all derived from American Methodism, though they exhibit many similarities in spirituality to the English type.

Missions

Thomas Coke began the missionary activities of British Methodism by his eloquence and ceaseless travels. The first area where missions took root was the West Indies; then came Sierra Leone and southern Africa. The Gold Coast, French West Africa, and Nigeria received missionaries not much later, though the climate in many parts of Africa took a toll of missionary lives.

In India converts were very few until about 1880, when a mass movement swept many thousand low-caste Indians in the south into the Methodist and other churches. In China missionary work had a checkered career, though there were mass movements there also. The last missionary left China in 1949. In Australia the Methodist Church began in 1815 and, like the Methodist Church in South Africa, became independent before the end of the 19th century. The movement toward autonomy became a flood after World War II; only a few small churches remain under the control of the Overseas Division of the church. Most of the autonomous churches negotiate for united churches in their countries; and the Church of South India, including Anglicans, Methodists, Congregationalists, and Presbyterians, has been in existence since 1947, and the Church of North India since 1970.

American Methodists have been equally enthusiastic for missionary activity, and their greater resources have carried them over still larger areas of the Earth's surface. North India, Mexico, and most of the other countries of Latin America, Cuba, Korea, Japan, Taiwan, and many parts of Africa possess Methodist churches of the American tradition. The movement toward autonomy took place more slowly in these areas than in the British sphere of influence. The General Conference of the United Methodist Church makes plans for combining fraternal relations among them with their newly found independence.

World Methodism

The two Methodist traditions diverged considerably for most of the 19th century but toward its end began to converge again. Ecumenical Methodist (since 1951 World Methodist) Conferences have been held regularly since 1888. The World Methodist Council represents some 80 churches.

Methodism in the World Church

In Britain the Methodist Church is the largest of the Free Churches; it is not a nonconformist church but stands between nonconformity and

Anglicanism, with affinities to both. In the United States it is closely aligned with the other non-Anglican Protestant denominations.[1]

Evangelicalism in England and the Colonies

Methodism

The evangelical, or Methodist (named from the use of methodical study and devotion), movement in England led by John Wesley was similar to the Pietist movement in Germany. While a fellow of Lincoln College, Oxford, Wesley organized a group of earnest Bible students, made a missionary expedition to Georgia, and became a friend of the Moravians. Like the Pietists he emphasized the necessity of conversion and devoted much of his life to evangelistic preaching in England. He did not intend any separation, but the parish system of the Church of England was incapable of adjustment to his plan of free evangelism and lay preachers. In 1744 Wesley held the first conference of his preachers; soon this became an annual conference, the governing body of the Methodist societies, and was given a legal constitution in 1784. The Methodist movement had remarkable success, especially where the Church of England was failing— in the industrial parishes, in the deep countryside, in little hamlets, and in hilly country, such as Wales, Cumberland, Yorkshire, and Cornwall. In 1768 Methodist emigrants in the American colonies opened a chapel in New York, and thereafter the movement spread rapidly in the United States. It also succeeded in French-speaking cantons of Switzerland.

The Methodist movement seized upon the emotional and spiritual conscience that Protestant orthodoxy neglected. It revived the doctrines of grace and justification and renewed the tradition of moral earnestness, which had once appeared in Puritanism but which had temporarily faded during the reaction against Puritanism in the middle and late 17th century. In England it slowly began to strengthen the tradition of free churchmanship, though for a century or more many English Methodists believed themselves to be much nearer the Anglican Church from which they had issued than any other body of English Protestants. Hymns— hitherto confined (except for metrical Psalms) to the Lutheran churches— were accepted in other Protestants bodies, such as the Church of England, the Congregationalists, and the Baptists as a result of the Methodist movement, which produced some of the most eminent hymn writers, such as Philip Doddridge (1702–51) and Charles Wesley (1707–88).

---

[1] *The Rev. Rupert E. Davies wrote this article on Methodism up to this point. Only the spelling of some words have been changed to American English.*

The Twenty Five Articles of Religion

The Twenty Five Articles of Religion is the creed that was prepared by John Wesley, founder of Methodism, for the Methodist church in the United States. The creed was accepted at the conference in Baltimore, Md., in 1784, when the Methodist Episcopal Church was formally organized.

The Twenty-five Articles was essentially an abridgment of the Thirty-nine Articles of the Church of England that excluded references to specifically English situations and went beyond the original in excluding the strict Calvinist interpretation of predestination, adopting instead a more general Lutheran view. In general, Wesley simplified and liberalized the Church of England creed. His own Arminian (based on the views of the 17th-century Dutch Reformed theologian Arminius) beliefs (i.e., that man can by his own *Will* accept or reject divine grace) were not explicitly stated in this creed.

A BRIEF BIOGRAPHY OF WESLEY

BIRTH AND EARLY YEARS

Born in Epworth, England in 1703 (June 17)

> Parents were Susanna and Samuel Wesley
> 10 out of 19 children survived
> John was the 15th child
> Charles was born on December 18, 1707
> > and died on March 29, 1788

Fire consumed the Epworth parsonage on February 9, 1709

EDUCATION

Charterhouse School (age 10)
Oxford University in 1720

> Graduated from Christ Church College, Oxford in 1724
> Ordained a Deacon September 19, 1725
> Priested on September 22, 1728
> Received a Teaching Fellowship at Lincoln College in 1726
> Curate (pastoral assistant) to his Father in Epworth (1727-29)

Returned to Oxford

Books that guided Wesley:

> *Imitation of Christ* by Thomas a Kempis
> *Holy Living and Dying* by Jeremy Taylor
> *A Serious Call to Holy Living* by William Law

The Oxford Student Group: Started by Charles Wesley

> Other Members:

> > Robert Kirkham,
> > William Morgan
> > George Whitefield

Activities of the Holy Club: A Covenant Community

> > Systematic Bible Study
> > Mutual Discipline
> > Frequent Communion
> > Visited prisoners
> > Comforted the sick

> > Names given to them:

> > > Holy Club
> > > Bible Moths
> > > Methodists
> > > Enthusiasts
> > > Sacramentalists

MISSIONARY YEARS

Missionary to Georgia from 1735 to 1737

> Departed for Georgia on the Simmonds on October (17) 21, 1735
> Charles went as secretary to James Oglethorpe
> Others who went to Georgia:

> > Charles Delamotte
> > Benjamin Ingham
> > George Whitefiled planned to join them later

Charles returned in 1736
John returned on February 1, 1738

The Love Affair with 18 year old Sophia Hopkey

SPIRITUAL EXPERIENCES

Charles had his experience on May 21, 1738
John had his experience on May 24, 1738
The Aldersgate Experience: Peter Böehler

Aldersgate was a place where devout Christians met to confess their sins to one another. The society that Wesley went to had only nine members present that night. Only three were educated.

1. James Hutton: Bookseller
2. John Shaw: Attorney
3. John Wesley: Clergy
4. John Bray: Mechanic
5. A Barber
6. A Barber
7. A Poulterer
8. A Clogmaker
9. A Barrel repairer

The Visit to Herrnhut (Moravian community led by Count Zinzendorf)

FIELD PREACHING

The Decision to Preach in the fields, homes, and marketplaces (1739)

George Whitefield was the first to preach in Bristol
Wesley preached his first open-air sermon on April 2, 1739

Opposition to Wesley was generated by his...

Unconventional methods
Plain speaking about personal and social sins (slavery)
Emphasis on the need for repentance
Emphasis on experiencing the grace of God

Wesley's original objective: to renew the Church of England

SOCIETIES AND CLASSES

Wesley found it necessary to organize his converts (1739)

> The first Society was formed on May 1, 1739
> Societies were formed mostly in the London-Bristol-Newcastle
>   Triangle
> Societies (1739) and Classes (1742)
> The First Conference of Methodist leaders in 1744
> Trips to Wales, Ireland, and Scotland

The First Methodist Buildings

> The Foundry (London in Late 1739)
> The New Room (Bristol)
> City Road Chapel (London)

Wesley's converts built chapels for their gatherings

> The first chapel was The New Room in Bristol

Wesley preached 40,000 sermons and traveled 250,000 miles

> Wesley traveled 5,000 miles a year
> Wesley preached 4 to 5 sermons a day

MARRIAGE

Wesley Married Mary Vazeille, a widow with 4 children in 1751 at 48

> She left him, but there was no divorce

THE SPLIT WITH THE ANGLICAN CHURCH

The Deed of Declaration in 1784

> Rules and regulations for the guidance of the Methodist
>   societies in America
> This widened the split with the Anglican Church

The Ordination of Elders in 1784

> Wesley appointed Thomas Coke to be a superintendent in the U.S.

This empowered Coke to ordain others
This was the biggest break with the Anglican Church
This was the birthday of the American Church

The English Church did not begin until after Wesley's death

DEATH

Wesley died on March 2, 1791 at 88

Buried in the graveyard of City Road Chapel, London
There is a memorial plaque in Westminster Abbey
Hostility with the Anglican Church subsided in his latter years

QUOTES FROM JOHN WESLEY

BIRTH AND EARLY YEARS

"Children, as soon as I am released, sing a psalm of praise to God." (Susanna Wesley's last words)

EDUCATION

"A year or two after, Mr. Law's 'Christian Perfection' and 'Serious Call' were put into my hands. These convinced me, more than ever, of the absolute impossibility of being half a Christian; and I determined, through his grace, (the absolute necessity of which I was deeply sensible of), to be all-devoted to God, to give him all my soul, my body, and my substance." (1729)

"O give me that book! At any price give me the book of God! I have it: here is knowledge enough for me. Let me be a man of one book."

"Let us now unite the two so long divided, knowledge and vital piety."

MISSIONARY YEARS

While John Wesley was in Georgia, August Spangenberg asked him, "John Wesley, do you know whether or not you are saved? After thinking about it he replied, "I hope I am." He believed in salvation by faith long before he was converted and he even preached the doctrine but he says following his conversion, "But still I fixed not this faith on its right object; I meant only faith in God, not faith in or through Christ."

One of the Moravians on board ship asked John Wesley the question: "Do you know Jesus?" Wesley replied by saying, "I know that he is the savior of the world." The Moravian answered that by saying, "Yes, but do you know him?"

"What have I learned myself in the meantime? Why (what I least expected), that I, who went to America to convert others, was never myself converted to God."

CONVERSIONS

The Conversion of Charles Wesley on his sickbed

Peter Bohler came to his bedside and asked him; "Do you hope to be saved?" Charles replied to him with a "Yes." Bohler then asked him, "For what reason do you hope it?" Charles said, "Because I have used my best endeavors to serve God. Peter walked out very disturbed, but on May 21, 1738, Wesley said from his sickbed after many tears and dejection; "I saw that by faith I stand."

"I don't care who writes the theological books, so long as I can write the hymns."

The Conversion of John Wesley at Aldersgate

"In the evening I went very unwillingly to a society in Aldersgate Street, where one was reading Luther's preface to the Epistle to the Romans. About a quarter to nine, while he was describing the change which God works in the heart through faith in Christ, I felt my heart strangely warmed. I felt I did trust in Christ, Christ alone for salvation; and an assurance was given me that he hath taken away my sins, even mine, and saved me from the law of sin and death.

I began to pray with all my might for those who had in a more especial manner despitefully used me and persecuted me. I then testified openly to all there, what I now first felt in my heart. But it was not long before the enemy suggested, 'This cannot be faith; for where is thy joy?' Then was I taught, that peace and victory over sin are essential to faith in the Captain of our salvation: But that, as to the transports of joy that usually attend the beginning of it, especially in those who have mourned deeply, God sometimes giveth, sometimes withholdeth them, according to the counsels of his own will.

After my return home, I was much buffeted with temptations; but cried out, and they fled away. They returned again and again. I as often lifted up my eyes, and He 'sent me help from his holy place.' And herein I found the difference between this and my former state chiefly consisted. I was striving, yea, fighting with all my might under the law, as well as under grace. But then I was sometimes, if not often, conquered; now, I was always conqueror."

FIELD PREACHING

"I could scarcely reconcile myself at first to this strange way—having been all my life (till very lately) so tenacious of every point relating to decency and order, that I should have thought the saving of souls almost a sin if it had not been done in a Church."

"I love a commodious room, a soft cushion and a handsome pulpit, but field preaching saves souls."

"I look upon all the world as my parish; thus far I mean that in whatever part of it I am, I judge it meet, right, and my bounden duty to declare unto all that are willing to hear the glad tidings of salvation." March 20, 1739

SOCIETIES AND CLASSES

"Our societies were formed from those who were wandering upon the dark mountains, that belonged to no Christian Church; but were awakened by the preaching of the Methodists, who had pursued them through the wilderness of this world to the Highways and the Hedges—to the Markets and the Fairs—to the Hills and the Dales—who set up the Standard of the Cross in the Streets and Lanes of the Cities, in the Villages, in the Barns, and Farmers' Kitchens, etc.—and all this done in such a way, and to such an extent, as never had been done before since the Apostolic Age."

"Give me a hundred preachers who fear nothing but sin, and desire nothing but God, and I care not a straw whether they be clergy or laymen, for such alone will shake the gates of hell and set up the kingdom of heaven on earth."

There was one condition for membership—that of desiring to flee from the wrath which is to come. No doctrinal tests were ever laid down. On the Methodists, Wesley said...

> "...do not impose, in order to their admission, any opinions whatever. Let them hold particular or general redemption, absolute or conditional decrees; let them be churchmen, or dissenters, Presbyterians or Independents, it is no obstacle. Let them choose one mode of baptism or another, it is no bar to their admission. The Presbyterian may be a Presbyterian still; the Independent and Anabaptist use his own mode of worship. So may the Quaker; and none will contend with him about it. They think and let think. One

condition, and one only, is required—a real desire to save the soul. Where this is, it is enough; they desire no more; they lay stress upon nothing else; they only ask, 'Is thy heart herein as my heart? If it be, give me thy hand.'"

The Methodist Covenant (1752)

- That we will not listen or willingly inquire after ill concerning one another;
- That, if we do hear any ill of each other, we will not be forward to believe it;
- That as soon as possible we will communicate what we hear by speaking or writing to the person concerned;
- That until we have done this, we will not write or speak a syllable of it to any other person;
- That neither will we mention it, after we have done this, to any other person;
- That we will not make any exception to any of these rules unless we think ourselves absolutely obliged in conference.

"Entire sanctification, or Christian Perfection, is neither more nor less than pure love—love expelling sin and governing both the heart and life of a child of God."

THE SPLIT WITH THE ANGLICAN CHURCH

"If the Methodist leave the Church of England, God will leave them."

"How easy now are Bishops made
    At man or woman's whim!
Wesley his hands on Coke hath laid,
    But who laid hands on him?" —Charles Wesley

"How can you, how dare you suffer yourself to be called Bishop? I shudder, I start, at the very thought! Men may call me a knave or a fool, a rascal, a scoundrel, and I am content: but they shall never by my consent call me Bishop! For my sake, for God's sake, for Christ's sake put a full end to this!" —John Wesley

"I am not afraid that the people called Methodists should ever cease to exist either in Europe or America. But I am afraid, lest they should only exist as a dead sect, having the form of religion without power. And this undoubtedly will be the case, unless they hold fast...the doctrine, spirit, and discipline with which they first set out."

DEATH

"Here lieth the body of John Wesley, a brand plucked out of the burning, who died of a consumption in the fifty-first year of his age, not leaving, after his debts are paid, ten pounds behind him; praying, God be merciful to me, an unprofitable servant." —November 26, 1753.

"The best of all, God is with us."

2. THE CLASS MEETINGS

A Brief Sketch of Beginnings
by Various Authors

The Class Meetings
by James T. Reuteler

A BRIEF SKETCH OF BEGINNINGS

THE BEGINNINGS IN ENGLAND

Methodism is marked by an acceptance of the doctrines of historic Christianity; by an emphasis on those doctrines that indicate the power of the Holy Spirit to confirm the faith of the believer and transform his personal life; by insistence that the heart of religion lies in personal relationship with God; by simplicity of worship; by the partnership of ordained ministers and laity in the worship and administration of the church; by a concern for the underprivileged and the betterment of social conditions; and (at least in its British form) by the formation of small groups for mutual encouragement and edification.

Rupert Davies

In 1742 the class-meeting was introduced. This turned out to be of "unspeakable usefulness", as Wesley recognized. (The name was simply the English form of the Latin *classis*, division, and carried with it no overtones of school.) The classes were rather larger in size than the bands and involved every member of the society. Their original purpose was to encourage Christian stewardship, since each member gave a penny a week to the funds. Then Wesley realized that the leaders were "the persons who may not only receive the contributions, but also watch over the souls of their brethren". The class system secured discipline as well as providing fellowship and pastoral care.

Christian education gained a new dimension with the introduction of Sunday schools. They were started in 1769 by a Methodist, Hannah Ball, and then developed and popularized by Robert Raikes, an Anglican layman. ... The Sunday school movement in Britain marked a step towards free education for all.

Skevinton Wood,
"The Methodists,",*Eerdman's Handbook to the History of Christianity* (Grand Rapids: *WM. B. Eerdman's Publishing Company, 1977)*, pp. 451 and 455.

THE BEGINNINGS IN THE UNITED STATES

Birth of the Church: December 24, 1784

Methodism in America owed its beginnings to immigrants from Ireland. Robert Strawbridge, a Methodist local preacher from Drumsna, Ireland, settled at Sam's Creek in Maryland. He opened his log cabin for services and formed a society not long after his arrival in 1760. Soon he began to evangelize the district and further societies were started.

About the same time another local preacher from Ireland, Philip Embury, arrived in New York and joined the Lutheran church. In 1765 his cousin, Mrs. Barbara Heck, prodded him to preach again and start a Methodist society. A British army officer, Thomas Webb, also lent a hand. He sent Wesley an account of what was happening and appealed for help. Volunteers were asked for at the Conference of 1769. Richard Boardman and Joseph Pilmoor offered to go.

The major figure in the founding of American Methodism was Francis Asbury. He came from Handsworth near Birmingham, and had been apprenticed to an iron smelter before joining the ranks of Wesley's itinerant preachers. In 1771 he responded to another call to help in America. He urged his colleagues in America to press to the frontiers in their evangelism. Wesley's other preachers returned to base in England during the Revolutionary War; Asbury alone remained.

Skevinton Wood,
"The Methodists," *Eerdman's Handbook to the History of Christianity* (Grand Rapids: *WM. B. Eerdman's Publishing Company, 1977)*, p. 452.

THE CLASS MEETINGS

The story begins with the Religious Societies in England, some of which were present in the Anglican and Moravian Churches.

The Religious Societies

A German Lutheran pastor, Dr. Anthony Horneck, was familiar with some small house groups that had met under the leadership of Jakob Philipp Spener, first in Frankfurt and then elsewhere in Germany. Their aim was to develop a more disciplined spiritual life. Horneck, who had settled in England, encouraged the development of similar Religious Societies there. Lay people organized these Societies in order to deepen their faith and discipleship. This caused some suspicion among the clergy, but the Societies were committed to deepening the spiritual life of the churches. To deal with this criticism, the Societies avoided meeting during the prescribed Sunday services.

The movement grew in London and spread to many other cities as well. Samuel Wesley was invited to preach to one of these Societies in 1698, and in 1701, he organized a Society in Epworth, with nine charter members. New members could be added, but they had to be approved by the group, and twelve was set as the maximum size of a Society. When the Society reached twelve, two members were set aside to start a new Society. This provided for expansion while maintaining the small size, which encouraged honest participation and direct conversation. While the primary purpose of the Religious Society at Epworth was to deepen the spirituality of its members, their statement of purpose was "to set up schools for the poor, wherein children (or if need be, adult persons) may be instructed in the fundamentals of Christianity…and to take care of the sick and other poor, and to afford them spiritual as well as corporal helps."

Since the Religious Societies were limited to men, Susanna Wesley adapted the model and began to hold what she called "enlarged family prayers" in the Epworth rectory in 1712. This was the religious environment in which John Wesley grew up.

There is no record of how long any of these Societies lasted, but we know something of the impact they had on early Methodism. The Religious Societies promoted the practical aspects of Christian discipleship and became increasingly involved in caring for the poor, relieving debt, visiting the sick, providing for orphans, and setting up schools. They were also open to Wesley's preaching when the local Anglican congregations closed their doors and pulpits to him.

The Holy Club

The next step in our historical sketch of the method in Methodism has to do with the Holy Club. In 1725, John Wesley dedicated himself to no longer be "half a Christian [but] to be all-devoted to God." Charles Wesley made a similar commitment. When Charles entered Oxford, he discovered some friends with similar interests, and they started meeting together on a regular basis. The date for the beginning of the Holy Club can be set at 1729. Upon his return to Oxford, John was glad to find a group of serious thinkers. As a faculty member he became the group's leader. The name we usually associate with this group is the "Holy Club," but as mentioned earlier, there were other names leveled at it, including "Methodist."

The Holy Club is usually viewed as an example of an Anglican Religious Society because it had rules which its members drew up, it followed the practice of the Societies in using the stated prayers of the Anglican tradition, and required regular attendance at the sacrament as a condition for membership. One of the more influential members of the Holy Club, John Clayton, opposed being identified as an Anglican Religious Society. He feared that such identification would water down their rigorous discipline based upon the early church in its first five centuries. The members of the Holy Club understood themselves as a disciplined renewal movement within the Anglican Church. Wesley later stated their goal as the "recovery of the faith and practice of primitive Christianity."

Members of the Holy Club were interested in reading and discussing the classics, but their motives were religious rather than intellectual. They prayed three times aloud during the day, stopped for silent prayer every hour; practiced all the ordinances of the church; and spent their time visiting the sick and imprisoned and conducting schools for the poor. "Methodists" was the mildest name applied to the Holy Club. It was said of them:

> By rule they eat, by rule they drink,
> Do all things else by rule, but think—
> Accuse their priests of loose behavior,
> To get more in the laymen's favor;
> Method alone must guide 'em all,
> Whence Methodists themselves they call.

We know the names of some of the members of the Holy Club. Besides John and Charles Wesley, there were George Whitefield, James Hervy, John Gambold, Westley Hall, and John Clayton. Hervey wrote a best seller in the eighteenth Century, John Gambold and Westley Hall were won over to Moravian quietist piety. Gambold became a Moravian bishop and broke off their common work with the Wesley's. Charles Wesley was also tempted by quietism, but it only lasted for three weeks. Others became faithful pastors in the Anglican Church. At its height, the Holy Club had as many as thirty men in it, but when the Wesley's were absent, it shrank to five. Not everyone in the Holy Club turned out to be religious. One of the members married one of Wesley's sisters and was pronounced by the historian of the club "an unmitigated scamp."

In 1735, Wesley was invited by Dr. John Burton, Trustee of the Georgia Colony and patron of the Society for the Propagation of the Gospel (S.P.G.), to transfer the Holy Club to Georgia to reach out to the Indians and Colonists. In September of that year the invitation was accepted and approved by the Georgia Society. It proved impossible to take the entire Holy Club to Georgia. Only three members were aboard the Simmonds when it sailed from Gravesend on October 21, 1735. They were John and Charles and Benjamin Ingham. A new recruit, Charles Delamotte, made a fourth. George Whitefield was still a student at Oxford and was not yet ordained. He promised to join them later. Wesley refers to the Holy Club in Savannah and says that "twenty or thirty persons met at my house" on Sunday afternoons and evenings, and Wednesday evenings, and spent "about an hour in prayer, singing, and mutual exhortation." But he had less success with the Holy Club in Georgia than he had at Oxford. The Georgia groups varied considerably in size and were difficult to discipline. The Holy Club in Georgia ended in failure, but that is another story.

The Holy Club at Oxford adopted strict disciplines for themselves in an effort to gain "inward and outward righteousness." Wesley believed that lukewarm Christianity was worse than open or willful sin. He and the other members of the Holy Club labored to bring every area of their lives under submission to Jesus Christ. They toiled at strict self-examination, rigorous spiritual disciplines, and sacrificial good works, yet the assurance of salvation eluded them. At the end of the experience in Georgia, Wesley found himself mired in what he called "a spiritual wilderness." It was a Religious Society meeting on Aldersgate Street in London that enabled him to find the assurance that he sought. It came not by his own efforts but by grace through faith. Charles had a similar experience of assurance a few days earlier, and so we can date the beginning of the next period in their lives at May 21st and May 24th in 1738.

The United Societies

Upon returning to London, Wesley became involved in the Fetter Lane Society formed on May 1, 1738 by the Anglicans, but finally dominated by the Moravians. He states that forty or fifty of them agreed to meet together every Wednesday evening for a free conversation, begun and ended with prayer. This was not to be a substitute for worship and the sacrament. Wesley eventually became the unofficial leader of the Fetter Lane Society, but his leadership was challenged by a Moravian from Bohemia who won a majority of its members over to the belief that the best way to have a spiritual blessing was through "stillness." That meant the refraining from all good works, all study, and all participation in the services of the churches, until the blessing came. Before the year was finished, it became clear that Wesley could not accommodate himself to such an idea. He tried to patch things up, but finally withdrew with those who agreed with him. The Fetter Lane Society was given up entirely to the Moravians. The two streams divided: the Moravians continued their work of testifying to the reality of the inner spiritual life, and the Methodists took upon themselves the task of proclaiming holiness to the multitudes.

One might say that Wesley took the best of the Anglican and Moravian Religious Societies and created the United or Methodist Societies. The first Methodist Society was formed in London in November of 1739. Wesley describes the event:

> In the latter end of the year 1739, eight or ten persons came to me in London, who appeared to be deeply convinced of sin, and earnestly groaning for redemption. They desired (as did two or three more the next day) that I would spend some time with them in prayer and advise them how to flee from the wrath to come, which they saw continually hanging over their heads. That we might have more time for this great work, I appointed a day when they might all come together, which from thenceforward they did every week, namely, on Thursday in the evening. To these, and as many more as desired to join with them (for their number increased daily) I gave those advices from time to time which I judged most needful for them; and we always concluded our meeting with prayer suited to their several necessities.

That was the rise of the first United or Methodist Society. Others followed in such places as Bristol, Kingswood, Newcastle, and many other parts of England, Scotland, and Ireland. Wesley carefully defined the purpose of the society as *"a company of men having the form and seeking the power of godliness, united in order to pray together, to receive the word of exhortation, and to watch over one another in love, that they may help each other to work our their salvation."*

The Voluntary Band Meetings

As the Methodist Societies grew, their small-group emphasis would have been lost if it had not been for the development of bands and classes, which became common subdivisions of the Societies. Let us take a closer look at the voluntary bands before proceeding to the required classes. We are doing this because the bands actually preceded the classes. Bands developed out of Moravian influences. They were small group units within Moravian congregations. Wesley adopted the format of the bands during his ministry in Savannah, and when he returned to England, he, along with the Moravians, incorporated them into the Fetter Lane Society. When the Fetter Lane Society was first organized, it was Anglican, but it subdivided into bands following the Moravian custom.

The bands were divided into single gender groups and according to marital status. Composed of from five to ten persons, bands met once and sometimes twice a week for singing, prayer, and spiritual conversation, in which each person was to "speak freely, plainly, and concisely as he can, the real State of his Heart, with the several Temptations and Deliverances, since the last Time of meeting." Their focus was spiritual growth and maturity. The size and nature of the band enabled its members to discuss common problems more freely, which would not have been possible in mixed company. Membership in the bands was strictly voluntary, band tickets were marked with a letter b, and leaders were chosen from within the group. Only about one in five Methodists took the step of joining a band. Since band meetings were not considered essential, they fell into disuse at an early date.

The Required Classes

The required Class Meeting, which became the most characteristic mark of Methodism, arose quite by accident. A loan had to be taken out in Bristol to build the New Room, one of the first Methodist Society chapels. Wesley met with some leaders and asked, "How shall we pay the debt upon the preaching-house?" Captain Foy gave the following answer, "Let everyone in the Society give a penny a week and it will easily be done." "But many of them," said one, "have not a penny to give." "True" replied the Captain, "then put ten or twelve of them to me. Let each of these give what they can weekly, and I will supply what is wanting." Others made the same offer, and so Wesley divided the Societies among them, assigning a class of about twelve to each of these, whom he called Class Leaders.

It was quickly discovered that as the Class Leaders visited their members to collect the contributions, that they performed a unique pastoral role. They were watching other one another in love. This was not only time consuming, but it presented some other problems. The weekly rounds were inconvenient because many Methodists lived as servants in houses where the master or mistress would not permit visitors. Even where such visits were allowed, they were unable to talk in private. This led to the next development in the evolution of classes. Instead of the leader visiting the members, a weekly meeting was set up, which brought the class together with the leader for prayer, Bible study, mutual confession and support. In addition to being a means of paying off a debt, the classes provided training in mutual accountability. Hence the twofold dynamic of the class meeting emerged: (1) watching over one another in love, and (2) holding one another mutually accountable.

It was not difficult to get into a class. It was indeed required of every person who wanted to belong to a Methodist Society. There was only one condition for persons who desired admission and that was "a desire to flee from the wrath to come, to be saved from their sins." As the classes developed it became clear that they needed some guidance, and so Wesley drew up the General Rules in 1743. The aim of the General Rules was to provide the Methodists with biblically prescribed guidelines for holy living. While the General Rules went through thirty-nine revisions in Wesley's lifetime, their outline remained essentially the same. It was expected of all who continued within the Methodist Societies that they give evidence of their desire of salvation:

> First, by doing no harm, by avoiding evil in every kind; especially that which is most generally practised.
> Second, by doing good, by being in every kind merciful after their power; as they have opportunity, doing good of every possible sort, and as far as is possible to all men....
> Thirdly, by attending upon all the ordinances of God. Such are the public worship of God; the ministry of the word, either read or expounded, the Supper of the Lord; private prayer, searching the Scriptures; and fasting, or abstinence.

Even a religious conversion was not required to enter a Class Meeting. In fact, more religious conversions occurred within the Class Meetings than in the public preaching services. Class Meeting activities were conducive to conversion. They included singing, prayer, and the sharing of spiritual struggles and victories. Class members were expected to follow the rule of confidentiality: "Let nothing spoken in this society be spoken again."

Wesley saw the support and encouragement provided by the Societies, bands, and classes as nothing other than the pattern provided by the apostles and the early church. He saw the class meetings not as an innovation of the Church, but the recovery of the basic principles for the practice of Christian discipleship. From 1745-1748, Wesley experimented with placing the emphasis on preaching alone. During that time he did not form Societies or require people to join the Class Meetings. The result was disastrous. "Almost all the seed has fallen by the wayside; there is scarce any fruit remaining," noted Wesley in the Minutes of the Conference of 1748. At that same Conference the decision was made to turn again to the formation of Societies with their Class Meetings.

Research done by Thomas Albin on the spiritual lives of five hundred fifty-five early British Methodists, whose spiritual biographies were published in the pages of the *Arminian Magazine* and the *Methodist Magazine*, shows that according to their own testimony, only one-fourth experienced new birth in the context of preaching. Three-fourths of them needed the nurture of the Society, classes, and bands, and spent an average of 2.3 years in this nurturing process before experiencing what they themselves identified as new birth. The Class Leaders and fellow class members were the primary influences. Because of this valuable truth, Methodist preaching at typical open-air meetings ended not with an *altar call* and a count of the number of conversions, but with an announcement of where the local Methodist Society met and an invitation to join one of the Class Meetings.

While profession of Christian conversion was not a requirement to be in a Methodist Class Meeting, classes only admitted serious seekers. Class Meeting tickets were issued quarterly first at Bristol and Kingswood to guard against "disorderly walkers," some forty of which were expelled in February of 1741. The issuing of tickets spread to London and other places for the same reason, to maintain the level of seriousness and accountability that characterized the Class Meetings. Similar tickets were issued to members of the bands. Three consecutive absences from the Class Meeting meant the loss of one's ticket, and without a ticket, one could not gain admission into the meetings. Class Leaders were required to keep an accurate record of attendance.

Just how many class were there? In 1766, the first year for which we have any statistics, they numbered approximately 19,000 in England and Wales. At Wesley's death in 1791, there were more than 53,000. The population of England and Wales at that time was between 8.5 and 9 million. In 1866, the Methodist Episcopal Church South discontinued the requirement of weekly attendance at Class Meetings. The Methodist Discipline continued to include instructions for Class Meetings until the

1930's. Regardless of what we have done with the Class Meetings today, it remains the most theological and practical contribution made by Wesley, and by Methodism to the Christian tradition. Wesley called them the prudential means of grace. If Wesley understood the Class Meetings as the sinew (muscle) of Methodism, what gives us the right to set them aside? Our problem today is that we think we have outgrown the snares of sinful human nature, but nothing could be further from the truth.

One might well ask, "If the Class Meeting was so important to the rise of Methodism, why was it ever given up?" Several reasons are given for the decline of the Class Meetings. The first is that the Methodist Societies became a church. For awhile the Class Meetings continued to energize the church; but soon pastors began to settle down in particular parishes, diminishing the need for Class Leaders. The second reason is that the Class Meetings simply gave way to Sunday School Classes. Listening to teachers interpret biblical passages became more popular than participation in Class Meetings where members were expected to share their spiritual journeys and be accountable to one another. The third reason had to do with the waning of the fires of revival. Class Meetings became perfunctory, and by the beginning of the twentieth century, the Class Meetings had all but disappeared, except where spirituality was alive and well, such as in the Black and Korean churches. They have also continued to exist in some third world churches, or among other denominations where the combination of spirituality and accountability is valued.

3. THE GENERAL RULES

The General Rules

The United Methodist Discipline

Discipline in the Christian Life

The Restrictive Rules

Questions for Becoming a Pastor

Knowing and Keeping the General Rules

THE GENERAL RULES

The General Rules are printed here in the text of 1808 (when the fifth Restrictive Rule took effect), as subsequently amended by constitutional actions in 1848 and 1868.

The Nature, Design, and General Rules of Our United Societies

In the latter end of the year 1739 eight or ten persons came to Mr. Wesley, in London, who appeared to be deeply convinced of sin, and earnestly groaning for redemption. They desired, as did two or three more the next day, that he would spend some time with them in prayer, and advise them how to flee from the wrath to come, which they saw continually hanging over their heads. That he might have more time for this great work, he appointed a day when they might all come together, which from thenceforward they did every week, namely, on Thursday in the evening. To these, and as many more as desired to join with them (for their number increased daily), he gave those advices from time to time which he judged most needful for them, and they always concluded their meeting with prayer suited to their several necessities.

This was the rise of the United Society, first in Europe, and then in America. Such a society is no other than "a company of men having the form and seeking the power of godliness, united in order to pray together, to receive the word of exhortation, and to watch over one another in love, that they may help each other to work out their salvation."

That it may the more easily be discerned whether they are indeed working out their own salvation, each society is divided into smaller companies, called classes, according to their respective places of abode. There are about twelve persons in a class, one of whom is styled the leader. It is his (or her) duty:

1. To see each person in his (or her) class once a week at least, in order:

    (1) to inquire how their souls prosper;

    (2) to advise, reprove, comfort or exhort, as occasion may require;

    (3) to receive what they are willing to give toward the relief of the preachers, church, and poor.

2. To meet the ministers and the stewards of the society once a week, in order:

(1) to inform the minister of any that are sick, or of any that walk disorderly and will not be reproved;

(2) to pay the stewards what they have received of their several classes in the week preceding.

There is only one condition previously required of those who desire admission into these societies: "a desire to flee from the wrath to come, and to be saved from their sins." But wherever this is really fixed in the soul it will be shown by its fruits.

It is therefore expected of all who continue therein that they should continue to evidence their desire of salvation,

First: By doing no harm, by avoiding evil of every kind, especially that which is most generally practiced, such as:

1. The taking of the name of God in vain.

2. The profaning the day of the Lord, either by doing ordinary work therein or by buying or selling.

3. Drunkenness: buying or selling spirituous liquors, or drinking them, unless in cases of extreme necessity.

4. Slaveholding; buying or selling slaves.

5. Fighting, quarreling, brawling, brother going to law with brother; returning evil for evil, or railing for railing; the using many words in buying or selling.

6. The buying or selling goods that have not paid the duty.

7. The giving or taking things on usury—i.e., unlawful interest.

8. Uncharitable or unprofitable conversation; particularly speaking evil of magistrates or of ministers.

9. Doing to others as we would not they should do unto us.

10. Doing what we know is not for the glory of God, as:

11. The putting on of gold and costly apparel.

12. The taking such diversions as cannot be used in the name of the Lord Jesus.

13. The singing those songs, or reading those books, which do not tend to the knowledge or love of God.

14. Softness and needless self-indulgence.

15. Laying up treasure upon earth.

16. Borrowing without a probability of paying; or taking up goods without a probability of paying for them.

It is expected of all who continue in these societies that they should continue to evidence their desire of salvation,

Secondly: By doing good; by being in every kind merciful after their power; as they have opportunity, doing good of every possible sort, and, as far as possible, to all men (persons):

1. To their bodies, of the ability which God giveth, by giving food to the hungry, by clothing the naked, by visiting or helping them that are sick or in prison.

2. To their souls, by instructing, reproving, or exhorting all we have any intercourse with; trampling under foot that enthusiastic doctrine that "we are not to do good unless our hearts be free to it."

3. By doing good, especially to them that are of the household of faith or groaning so to be; employing them preferably to others; buying one of another, helping each other in business, and so much the more because the world will love its own and them only.

4. By all possible diligence and frugality, that the gospel be not blamed.

5. By running with patience the race which is set before them, denying themselves, and taking up their cross daily; submitting to bear the reproach of Christ, to be as the filth and offscouring of the world; and looking that men (or women) should say all manner of evil of them falsely, for the Lord's sake.

It is expected of all who desire to continue in these societies that they should continue to evidence their desire of salvation,

Thirdly: By attending upon all the ordinances of God; such are:

1. The public worship of God.

2. The ministry of the Word, either read or expounded.

3. The Supper of the Lord.

4. Family and private prayer.

5. Searching the Scriptures.

6. Fasting or abstinence.

These are the General Rules of our societies; all of which we are taught of God to observe, even in his written Word, which is the only rule, and the sufficient rule, both of our faith and practice. And all these we know his Spirit writes on truly awakened hearts. If there be any among us who observe them not, who habitually break any of them, let it be known unto them who watch over that soul as they who must give an account. We will admonish him (or her) of the error of his (or her) ways. We will bear with him (or her) for a season. But then, if he (or she) repent not, he (or she) hath no more place among us. We have delivered our own souls.

DISCIPLINE IN THE CHRISTIAN LIFE

No motif in the Wesleyan tradition has been more constant than the link between Christian doctrine and Christian living. Methodists have always been strictly enjoined to maintain the unity of faith and good works through the means of grace, as seen in John Wesley's The Nature, Design, and General Rules of the United Societies (1743). The coherence of faith with ministries of love forms the discipline of Wesleyan spirituality and Christian discipleship.

The General Rules were originally designed for members of Methodist societies who participated in the sacramental life of the Church of England. The terms of membership in these societies were simple: "a desire to flee from the wrath to come and to be saved from their sins."

Wesley insisted, however, that evangelical faith should manifest itself in evangelical living. He spelled out this expectation in the three-part formula of the Rules:

It is therefore expected of all who continue therein that they should continue to evidence their desire of salvation,

First: By doing no harm, by avoiding evil of every kind . . . ;
Secondly: By . . . doing good of every possible sort, and, as far as possible, to all . . . ;
Thirdly: By attending upon all the ordinances of God (see ¶ 62).

Wesley's illustrative cases under each of these three rules show how the Christian conscience might move from general principles to specific actions. Their explicit combination highlights the spiritual spring of moral action.

Wesley rejected undue reliance upon these rules. Discipline was not church law; it was a way of discipleship. Wesley insisted that true religion is "the knowledge of God in Christ Jesus," "the life which is hid with Christ in God," and "the righteousness that [the true believer] thirsts after."

THE RESTRICTIVE RULES

¶ 16. Article I. —The General Conference shall not revoke, alter, or change our **Articles of Religion** or establish any new standards or rules of doctrine contrary to our present existing and established standards of doctrine.32

Article II. —The General Conference shall not revoke, alter, or change our **Confession of Faith**.

¶ 17. Article III. —The General Conference shall not change or alter any part or rule of our government so as to do away with the **episcopacy** or destroy the plan of our itinerant **general superintendency**.

¶ 18. Article IV.—The General Conference shall not do away with the privileges of our clergy of right to trial by a committee and of an appeal; neither shall it do away with the privileges of our members of right to trial before the church, or by a committee, and of an appeal.

¶ 19. Article V.—The General Conference shall not revoke or change the **General Rules** of Our United Societies.

¶ 20. Article VI.—The General Conference shall not appropriate the net **income of the publishing houses**, the book concerns, or the Chartered Fund to any purpose other than for the benefit of retired or disabled preachers, their spouses, widows, or widowers, and children or other beneficiaries of the ministerial pension systems.

QUESTIONS FOR BECOMING A PASTOR

Historic Examination for Admission into Full Connection and Ordination as Deacon—The bishop as chief pastor shall engage those seeking to be admitted in serious self-searching and prayer to prepare them for their examination before the conference. At the time of the examination, the bishop shall also explain to the conference the historic nature of the following questions and seek to interpret their spirit and intent. The questions are these and any others which may be thought necessary:

(1)   Have you faith in Christ?
(2)   Are you going on to perfection?
(3)   Do you expect to be made perfect in love in this life?
(4)   Are you earnestly striving after perfection in love?
(5)   Are you resolved to devote yourself wholly to God and God's work?
(6)   Do you know the **General Rules** of our Church?
(7)   Will you keep the **General Rules** of our Church?
(8)   Have you studied the doctrines of The United Methodist Church?
(9)   After full examination do you believe that our doctrines are in harmony with the Holy Scriptures?
(10) Have you studied our form of Church discipline and polity?
(11) Do you approve our Church government and polity?
(12) Will you support and maintain them?
(13) Will you exercise the ministry of compassion?
(14) Will you recommend fasting or abstinence, both by precept and example?
(15) Are you determined to employ all your time in the work of God?
(16) Are you in debt so as to embarrass you in your work?
(17) Will you observe the following directions?

(a) Be diligent. Never be unemployed. Never be triflingly employed. Never trifle away time; neither spend any more time at any one place than is strictly necessary.
(b) Be punctual. Do everything exactly at the time. And do not mend our rules, but keep them; not for wrath, but for conscience' sake.

4. THE NEW GENERAL RULE

The Method in Methodism
James T. Reuteler

The New General Rule
David Watson, Edited by James T. Reuteler

Covenant Discipleship Groups Graphic
David Watson

THE METHOD IN METHODISM

Why not let things alone? Maybe we do not need Class Meetings in modern Methodism. If we were taking Christian discipleship as seriously today as the early Christians and early Methodists did, then our conclusion might be to move in new and different directions. When we look at early Methodism, we find that they were more interested in obedience to Christ than they were in doctrinal beliefs, or even religious experience. Class Leaders were charged with the task of making sure that this priority was upheld. This meant accountability, the one thing missing in modern Methodism.

The above is well illustrated in how The United Methodist Church deals with membership. In our effort to attract more members, we emphasize the benefits of membership and downplay the cost of discipleship. This is a direct inversion of the invitation to discipleship given by Jesus, who allows people unwilling to pay the price to simply walk away. We are consumed with membership enrollment, or at least increasing our average attendance. This comes dangerously close to idolatry. The consequence of this approach is that we compromise the cost of discipleship in order to attract more people into membership or to warm our pews. A true response to Christ does result in benefits, but not without the cost of discipleship.

How did we come to this? It happened quite naturally as we did away with the *method* in Methodism—the Class Meeting. We moved away from what James D. Anderson and Ezra Earl Jones calls transformational leadership. The business model of transactional leadership was adopted. David Watson defines the difference in these two kinds of leadership:

> Transactional leadership is responsible for meeting the needs of church members, and for the institutional maintenance of the church. Transformational leadership is responsible for keeping church members focused on the vision of the gospel and the obligations of their discipleship.

Both kinds of leadership are necessary, but both kinds of leadership need to be given distinct and equal emphasis in the life and mission of the church. In early Methodism that balance was maintained with two kinds of leaders—the Class Leaders and the Stewards. Class Leaders focused on forming disciples and Stewards focused on the care of temporal things. We have our equivalence of Stewards in our committee structure which does a fairly good job of administrating the church, but we have nothing like the Class Leaders who kept Methodism focused on forming disciples, even though we claim that our primary mission is "to make disciples." We need to restore something like the Class Meeting in order to develop transformational leaders. We already have plenty of transactional leaders. We know how to transact business, but we do not know how to make disciples.

Covenant Discipleship Groups. There is no point in reinventing the wheel, if do not have to. Fortunately, David Lowes Watson developed what he named "Covenant Discipleship Groups" at Holly Springs United Methodist Church in Holly Springs, North Carolina in 1975. At the time the members of Holly Springs United Methodist Church did not know they were doing anything particularly significant. They just wanted to seek the grace of God by practicing the disciplines of the faith, and to hold one another accountable for their discipleship. In doing this they reestablished both accountability and transformational leadership. They learned how to make disciples, the primary mission of The United Methodist Church. They were theologically driven; whereas, most congregations are sociologically driven. Transactional leaders try to please the members rather than move them to pay the cost of Christian discipleship. For example, the only condition of discipleship that one can find in the New Testament is Jesus' call to obedience, to carry a cross. There is never any discussion of potential benefits, even though they existed.

Watson defines both the Class Meeting of the past and Covenant Discipleship Groups in modern Methodism. Let us look first at his definition of the Class Meeting, which is:

> The class meeting was a weekly gathering, a subdivision of the early societies, at which members were required to give an account to one another of their discipleship and thereby to sustain each other in their witness. These meetings were regarded by Wesley as the "sinews" of the Methodist movement, the means by which members "watched over one another in love."

Two things happened in those early class meetings that can and should be done today—accountability and the watching over of one another in love.

Through the class meetings, Wesley called the church back to the principles of scriptural Christianity, personal holiness, and social responsibility; and he did this through the ordinances of the Church. This was the method in Methodism, and we still need it in some form today. Covenant Discipleship Groups represent a modern approach to the Class Meetings of early Methodism. Watson's definition follows:

> A covenant discipleship group consists of two to seven people who agree to meet together for one hour per week in order to hold themselves mutually accountable for their discipleship. They do

this by affirming a written covenant on which they themselves have agreed.

While the group may have as few as two members, the dynamic of the meeting is impeded. The dynamic is much better with four to seven members. Eight members is generally considered too many because the larger number limits conversation. The larger number might be used when a group member travels or finds it difficult to meet every week.

Watson estimates that 15% of the active membership or 5-7% of the total membership in a United Methodist Church are ready to take part in Covenant Discipleship Groups. As such groups are formed, there are a few principles that need to be understood.

1. The pastor should be involved. The most natural support group for the pastor is not other pastors, but the pastor's own people.

2. The staff should be involved, but they should not be expected to provide permanent leadership, even though they may well provide such leadership in the beginning.

3. Discipleship groups should last one hour, and they should start and finish on time.

4. A new member may visit three times. Then he or she must decide whether or not to join the group.

5. There are regular opportunities for changing the covenant, but welcoming a new member is not one of them.

6. Covenant Sunday is a good time for groups to review their meeting schedules, revise their covenants, and if necessary, change groups.

7. The accountability of the groups is for the purpose of the forming of faithful disciples and holding them on course as they live out their discipleship in the world. Covenant Discipleship Groups are not to be used as work groups for repairing or building things around the church.

The New General Rule. While the modern name for the Class Meeting is the Covenant Discipleship Group, the modern name for the General Rules is the New General Rule or The General Rule of Discipleship. The General Rules written up by Wesley contained not only the obligations of discipleship, but how those obligations were to be carried out by the classes. Wesley's intent was to help the members of the Class Meetings maintain a balance in their discipleship; therefore, the

General Rules were three in number: to do no harm, to do good, and to participate in all of the ordinances of the church. Each of these three rules contained a number of specific clauses, some of which are not relevant today. The ordinances of the church are very much the same as today. They include: prayer, the searching of the scriptures, the Lord's Supper, fasting and abstinence, and Christian conferencing. Only the last two need some explanation to make them relevant to modern times. Fasting and abstinence was suggested in order to help people detach themselves from earthly things and to focus on spiritual realities. That was as much of a problem then as it is today. Christian conferencing refers to the importance of Christian community. In fellowship with others, we benefit from mutual accountability and growth.

Watson wants us to appreciate the historical General Rules, but he creates a New General Rule of Discipleship for today, which is:

To witness to Jesus Christ in the world,
and to follow his teachings through
acts of compassion, justice, worship, and devotion,
under the guidance of the Holy Spirit.

THE NEW GENERAL RULE

Witnessing

The primary mission of every Christian is to bear witness to Jesus Christ, not in the church, but in the world. Wesley said that God raised up the Methodists "...not to form any new sect; but to reform the nation, particularly the Church; and to spread scriptural holiness over the land." When the Anglican Church accused him of proselytizing, he replied:

> Our societies were formed from those who were wandering upon the dark mountains, that belonged to no Christian Church; but were awakened by the preaching of the Methodists, who had pursued them through the wilderness of this world to the Highways and the Hedges—to the Markets and the Fairs—to the Hills and the Dales —who set up the Standard of the Cross in the Streets and Lanes of the Cities, in the Villages, in the Barns, and Farmers' Kitchens, etc. — and all this done in such a way, and to such an extent, as never had been done before since the Apostolic Age.

The early Methodists discovered scripture and prayer in the early Class Meetings. They also found their voice and felt impelled to witness. The rapid growth of Methodism was attributable to that witnessing. Wesley insisted that "...our calling is to save that which is lost. Now, we cannot expect the wanderers from God to seek us. It is our part to go and seek them." The purpose of the church must be given as much priority today as it was in early Methodism. We need to gather in Covenant Discipleship Groups to plan our strategy for witnessing in the world and hold one another accountable for it. Our greatest witness will focus on works of mercy and works of piety.

Works of Mercy

In works of mercy, disciples are to do everything possible to serve God and their neighbor, while at the same time avoiding those things that offend God and harm their neighbor. In the New General Rule there are two works of mercy—acts of compassion and acts of justice. Compassion is a private act and justice is a public act. Watson defines acts of compassion as follows:

> Acts of compassion are those simple, basic things we do out of kindness to our neighbor; and our neighbor is anyone who is in need, anywhere in the world. To the extent that we feed the hungry, clothe the naked, and visit the sick and the imprisoned, we minister to Christ in our midst.

The primary scriptural passages to support our need to witness through acts of compassion can be found in the last judgement in Matthew 25:31-46; the parable of the Good Samaritan in Luke 10:25-37; and in James 2:14-17.

Justice is a social act. Wesley did not take the Methodist societies out of the world, but showed them how to follow God in the world. He knew that they would be marked people for declaring publicly that the personal and social teachings of Jesus were to be taken seriously. To pattern their lives after Jesus would lead to considerable tension with the world in which they lived. Watson defines acts of justice as follows:

> Acts of justice remind us that God thundered the law from Sinai and pronounced righteousness through the prophets. We must not only minister to people in need, but ask why they are in need in the first place. And if they are being treated unjustly, then we must confront the persons or systems that cause the injustice.

The primary scriptural passages to support our need to witness through acts of justice are the Old Testament prophets, specifically Amos 5:24, and Jesus opening sermon in Nazareth, which is located in Luke 4:16-21.

Why do we need to be held accountable for acts of compassion and justice? Wesley knew all too well that the promptings of the Holy Spirit could be ignored or misinterpreted due to laziness. Works of mercy are obligatory for Christians, even if they are not in the mood for them. The hungry need feeding, even if we are not in the mood to feed them. The naked need to be clothed, whether or not it is convenient for us. The sick need help, whether or not we are feeling up to it. Those in prison need to be visited, whether or not we feel we have anything to offer them. Acts of compassion require acts of justice to follow. Most Covenant Discipleship Groups will have the most difficulty with acts of justice.

Works of Piety

In works of piety, disciples are to do everything needful to be open to God's grace. In the New General Rule there are two works of piety—acts of devotion and acts of worship. Acts of devotion are private and acts of worship are public. Watson defines acts of devotion as follows.

> Acts of devotion are those private spiritual disciplines of prayer, reading the scriptures, and inward examination, that bring us face to face with God most directly, when no one else is present. At such times, our dialogue with God is intensely personal, searching, and enriching.

The four most personal acts of devotion would be searching the scripture, prayer, fasting, and giving. Scriptural passages that support these devotions include 2 Timothy 13:4-17; Matthew 6:4-15; Matthew 6:16-18; and Matthew 6:19-21. For a better understanding of fasting, look up Isaiah 58:6-10. Obviously, acts of devotion lead us into acts of worship, the public expression of the works of piety.

In acts of worship we observe the ordinances of the Church, or what might be called the means of grace in a public manner. Wesley insisted that Methodists ought to participate in the Lord's Supper as frequently as they can. In the early days, the Methodist services avoided offering the Lord's Supper because Wesley was encouraging everyone to worship on Sunday in the nearest Anglican Church. Methodism was to be a *method* of carrying out one's discipleship. It was not to become a Church. Watson defines the acts of worship as follows:

> Acts of worship are the means of grace that we exercise corporately: the ministries of word and sacrament. Not only do they affirm the indispensable place of the church in Christian discipleship. They also enable us to build each other up in the Body of Christ.

Our regularity of worship in word and sacrament is far more important than the benefits we might derive from them. Our presence is itself a witness. To become more regular in worship we need to be accountable to one another. We need each other to discern the will of God. No one can do this on his or her own. The important scriptural passages that support our witness through acts of worship might include Matthew 18:20; Acts 2:41-47; and Hebrews 10:22-25.

The Guidance of the Holy Spirit

All of the above is to be done under the guidance of the Holy Spirit. Christian disciples, insists Watson, do not have *bright ideas;* they have *promptings* from the Holy Spirit. Christian disciples do not *have twinges of conscience*; they have *warnings* from the Holy Spirit. Identifying these *promptings* and *warnings* is one of the critical tasks of every Covenant Discipleship Group. The guidance of the Holy Spirit is best comprehended where two or three are gathered together seeking it. It is too easy for the individual to ignore the *promptings* and *warnings* of the Holy Spirit.

To understand how the Holy Spirit operates in our lives, it might be helpful to look more carefully at Wesley's religious experience at Aldersgate. Wesley describes when it happened (*a quarter before nine, while he was describing the change which God works in the heart through faith in Christ*), but he also recounts the impression made on his spiritual senses (*I felt my heart strangely warmed. I felt I did trust in Christ, Christ alone for salvation: And an assurance was given me, that he had taken away my sins, even mine, and saved me from the law of sin and death*). The primary actor at Aldersgate was the Holy Spirit making an impression on Wesley's mind and heart.

The Holy Spirit works through our spiritual senses. "To every other eye," said Rudolf Bultmann, "other than the eye of faith the action of God is hidden." So, what are these spiritual senses through which the Holy Spirit guides us? Archbishop William Temple alluded to the spiritual senses when he defined worship. "To worship," he wrote, "is to quicken the *conscience* by the holiness of God, to feed the *mind* with the truth of God, to purge the *imagination* by the beauty of God, to open the *heart* to the love of God, to devote the *will* to the purpose of God." Drawing upon Temple's definition of worship, I would suggest the following spiritual senses: (1) reflective reason, (2) common sense, (3) a moral conscience, (4) free choice, and (5) feelings of the heart. All of these spiritual senses put together make the individual able to respond to God's gift of grace (unmerited love) by faith (Ephesians 2:8-9). We could certainly spend time with each of the spiritual senses, but discussion of one should suffice. Wesley rejected the idea of a natural conscience. Conscience, he insisted, is a gift from God. What we all have is a moral sense, but we must be careful that we do not destroy that moral sense. Wesley's own experience of assurance occurred not in solitude, but in the company of fellow believers. Sharpening our spiritual senses depends upon being accountable to fellow believers. Without that accountability, we are likely to make shipwreck not only of our conscience, but also of our souls. Some important scriptural passages that support the impression that the Holy Spirit makes on us to guide us can be found in Romans 8:12-16 and 1 Timothy 1:18-19.

Two Testimonies

I know that the discipleship covenant changed my life. Just yesterday I was looking over my commitments made in the acts of compassion, justice, worship and devotion. I was amazed at what has been accomplished since the publication of this covenant, which for me occurred October 28, 2000.

In the act of compassion, my prison ministry began six weeks later. I have learned very valuable lessons from this ministry that have served to help me work through the other acts. One lesson I learned was to overcome my feeling of lack of qualification for this ministry, the Spirit guides me every time I work with the inmates. Secondly, I have found the courage I thought I lacked. ***Pat Bruhn***

Missed the meeting last week due to a mini-vacation—it's amazing how much that hour means to me. ***Krista Sperger***

COVENANT DISCIPLESHIP GROUPS

A Covenant Discipleship Group consists of up to seven people who agree to meet together for one hour each week in order to hold themselves mutually accountable for their discipleship. They do this by affirming a written covenant on which they themselves have agreed.

The General Rule of Discipleship

While each group writes its own covenant in the context of its members' discipleship, all covenants are shaped by a General Rule, patterened after John Wesley's General Rules.

To witness to Jesus Christ in the world, and to follow his teachings through acts of compassion, acts of justice, acts of worship, and acts of devotion, under the guidance of the Holy Spirit.

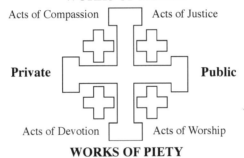

WORKS OF MERCY

Acts of Compassion ⸺ Acts of Justice

Private ⸺ **Public**

Acts of Devotion ⸺ Acts of Worship

WORKS OF PIETY

Mutual Accountability

At the weekly meetings of the group, each member gives an account of her or his discipleship during the past week in light of the covenant. This is done by responding to the questions of the leader for the week, who addresses each clause of the covenant in turn. The role of leader rotates, giving everyone in the group a shared opportunity and responsibility.

5. THE TRINITY

The Methodist Articles of Religion

I through IV

The Evangelical United Brethren Confession of Faith

Articles 1 through 4

The Articles of Faith

I through IV

Misunderstandings of the Trinity

The Misunderstandings

The Trinity

A Diagram of the Trinity

THE METHODIST ARTICLES OF RELIGION
I through IV

Bibliographical Note: The Articles of Religion are here reprinted from the Discipline of 1808 (when the first Restrictive Rule took effect), collated against Wesley's original text in The Sunday Service of the Methodists (1784). To these are added two Articles: "Of Sanctification" and "Of the Duty of Christians to the Civil Authority," which are legislative enactments and not integral parts of the document as protected by the Constitution (see Judicial Council Decisions 41, 176).

Article I—Of Faith in the Holy Trinity

There is but one living and true God, everlasting, without body or parts, of infinite power, wisdom, and goodness; the maker and preserver of all things, both visible and invisible. And in unity of this Godhead there are three persons, of one substance, power, and eternity—the Father, the Son, and the Holy Ghost.

Article II—Of the Word, or Son of God, Who Was Made Very Man

The Son, who is the Word of the Father, the very and eternal God, of one substance with the Father, took man's nature in the womb of the blessed Virgin; so that two whole and perfect natures, that is to say, the Godhead and Manhood, were joined together in one person, never to be divided; whereof is one Christ, very God and very Man, who truly suffered, was crucified, dead, and buried, to reconcile his Father to us, and to be a sacrifice, not only for original guilt, but also for actual sins of men.

Article III—Of the Resurrection of Christ

Christ did truly rise again from the dead, and took again his body, with all things appertaining to the perfection of man's nature, wherewith he ascended into heaven, and there sitteth until he return to judge all men at the last day.

Article IV—Of the Holy Ghost

The Holy Ghost, proceeding from the Father and the Son, is of one substance, majesty, and glory with the Father and the Son, very and eternal God.

THE EVANGELICAL UNITED BRETHREN CONFESSION OF FAITH

I through III

Bibliographical Note: The text of the Confession of Faith is identical to that of its original in The Discipline of The Evangelical United Brethren Church (1963).

Article I — God

We believe in the one true, holy and living God, Eternal Spirit, who is Creator, Sovereign and Preserver of all things visible and invisible. He is infinite in power, wisdom, justice, goodness and love, and rules with gracious regard for the well-being and salvation of men, to the glory of his name. We believe the one God reveals himself as the Trinity: Father, Son and Holy Spirit, distinct but inseparable, eternally one in essence and power.

Article II — Jesus Christ

We believe in Jesus Christ, truly God and truly man, in whom the divine and human natures are perfectly and inseparably united. He is the eternal Word made flesh, the only begotten Son of the Father, born of the Virgin Mary by the power of the Holy Spirit. As ministering Servant he lived, suffered and died on the cross. He was buried, rose from the dead and ascended into heaven to be with the Father, from whence he shall return. He is eternal Savior and Mediator, who intercedes for us, and by him all men will be judged.

Article III — The Holy Spirit

We believe in the Holy Spirit who proceeds from and is one in being with the Father and the Son. He convinces the world of sin, of righteousness and of judgment. He leads men through faithful response to the gospel into the fellowship of the Church. He comforts, sustains and empowers the faithful and guides them into all truth.

THE ARTICLES OF FAITH
I through IV

Note: When The Evangelical United Brethren and The Methodist Churches merged in 1968, they each had separate statements of faith. In The Evangelical United Brethren Church the statement was called the Confession of Faith, and in The Methodist Church the statement was called the Articles of Religion. In the Articles of Faith that Follow I have merged these two documents together. Articles 1-25 represent the Methodist Articles of Religion and the inclusion of the Evangelical United Brethren Confession of Faith where they have a parallel to the traditional Methodist Articles. Articles 26-27 come from the Evangelical United Brethren Confession of Faith, but represent traditional Methodist beliefs as well.

1. The Trinity

We believe there is but one living and true God, who is Creator and Preserver of all things visible and invisible. This one God is known in the three persons of the Trinity: Father, Son, and Holy Spirit, distinct but inseparable, eternally one in essence and power. Infinite in power, wisdom, goodness, and love, this God rules with gracious regard for the well-being and salvation of all persons.

2. Jesus Christ

We believe in the Son, who is the Word of the Father and of one being with the Father, took on human nature in the womb of the Virgin Mary by the power of the Holy Spirit. In him both the divine and human natures were joined together in one person. That person lived, suffered, and died on a cross to reconcile us all to the Father. In his sacrifice not only is the original sin of humanity forgiven, but all our particular sins as well.

3. The Resurrection of the Dead

We believe that Christ rose in bodily form from the dead and ascended into heaven where he will judge all persons on the last day; the righteous to life eternal and the wicked to endless condemnation.

4. The Holy Spirit

We believe that the Holy Spirit proceeds from and is one in being with the Father and the Son. He makes us aware of sin, of righteousness, and of judgment; and he leads us into a faithful response to the Gospel and into the fellowship of the Church. He comforts, sustains, and empowers the faithful, and guides us into all truth.

MISUNDERSTANDINGS
OF THE TRINITY

1. **TRI-THEISTS** (Christian Polytheism). Father, Son, and Holy Spirit represent three deities.

2. **UNITARIANISM** (Christian Judaism or Christian Islam). The Father alone is God. Jesus Christ is a special man who reveals the Father, and the Holy Spirit is a power, rather than a divine person.

The core of the doctrine of the trinity was and is the divinity of Christ. It springs not from philosophical speculation, but from historical understanding.

THE BIBLE

The Old Testament maintains the unity of God. There is only one God.

1. **Old Testament Images**

    • Man/Woman in our Image
    • Man/Woman has become like one of us
    • Whom shall I send and who will go for us

2. **New Testament Images**

    • Jesus' Baptism
    • Jesus' Temptation
    • The Great Commission
    • Paul's Benediction

"God's Spirit is God acting." —Alan Richardson (The Holy Spirit is not a divine power, but a divine person)

HERESIES

1. **Sabellianism/Modalism.** The Father, Son, and Spirit are "modes" of revelation, but in the essence of his Being, God is one.

2. **Arianism.** Only the Father is God. Jesus Christ is a created being. The Holy Spirit is a power or attribute of God.

THE TRINITY

God is one divine essence (substance or being) existing in three persons.

"When one asks: What three? human speech suffers from a great lack of power. Nevertheless, we say: Three persons, not in order that we should say this, but that we should not be silent."

Augustine

God not only reveals himself as Father, Son, and Holy Spirit; God is Father, Son, and Holy Spirit.

"Without the Spirit it is not possible to hold the Word of God nor without the Son can any draw near to the Father, for the knowledge of the Son of God is through the Holy Spirit."

Irenaeus of Lyons

"Since there is but one divine Being, why do you speak of three, Father, Son and Holy Spirit?" Answer: "Because God has revealed himself in his Word that these three distinct persons are the one, true and eternal God."

Heidelberg Catechism

THE IMPORTANCE OF THE TRINITY

1. **Revelation.** In the revelation of the Father in the Son through the Spirit we not only receive some information about God, but we have the assurance that God himself is speaking to us.

2. **Salvation.** The Trinity assures us that God really saves us in Christ. The Trinity assures us that our salvation has its foundation in the heart of God himself.

A DIAGRAM OF THE TRINITY

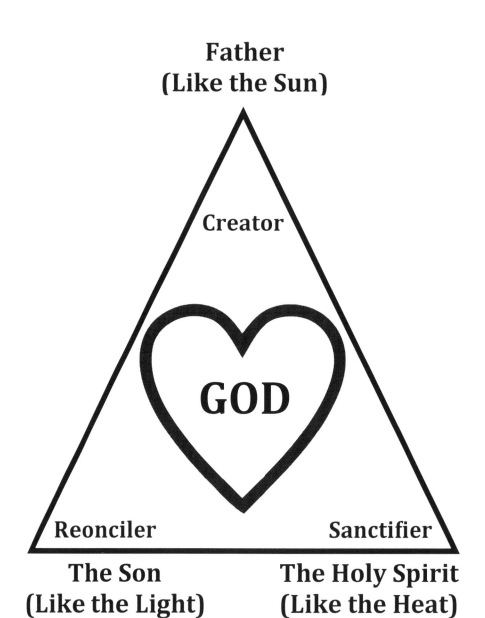

Father
(Like the Sun)

Creator

GOD

Reonciler

Sanctifier

The Son
(Like the Light)

The Holy Spirit
(Like the Heat)

6. SCRIPTURE

The Methodist Articles of Religion

V through VI

The Evangelical United Brethren Confession of Faith

IV

The Articles of Faith

5 through 6

The Wesley Quadrilateral

Scripture and Tradition

Variations

Schools of Interpretation

Three Main Types

THE METHODIST ARTICLES OF RELIGION

Article V — Of the Sufficiency of the Holy Scriptures for Salvation

The Holy Scripture containeth all things necessary to salvation; so that whatsoever is not read therein, nor may be proved thereby, is not to be required of any man that it should be believed as an article of faith, or be thought requisite or necessary to salvation. In the name of the Holy Scripture we do understand those canonical books of the Old and New Testament of whose authority was never any doubt in the church. The names of the canonical books are:

Genesis, Exodus, Leviticus, Numbers, Deuteronomy, Joshua, Judges, Ruth, The First Book of Samuel, The Second Book of Samuel, The First Book of Kings, The Second Book of Kings, The First Book of Chronicles, The Second Book of Chronicles, The Book of Ezra, The Book of Nehemiah, The Book of Esther, The Book of Job, The Psalms, The Proverbs, Ecclesiastes or the Preacher, Cantica or Songs of Solomon, Four Prophets the Greater, Twelve Prophets the Less.

All the books of the New Testament, as they are commonly received, we do receive and account canonical.

Article VI — Of the Old Testament

The Old Testament is not contrary to the New; for both in the Old and New Testament everlasting life is offered to mankind by Christ, who is the only Mediator between God and man, being both God and Man. Wherefore they are not to be heard who feign that the old fathers did look only for transitory promises. Although the law given from God by Moses as touching ceremonies and rites doth not bind Christians, nor ought the civil precepts thereof of necessity be received in any commonwealth; yet notwithstanding, no Christian whatsoever is free from the obedience of the commandments which are called moral.

THE EVANGELICAL UNITED BRETHREN
CONFESSION OF FAITH

Article IV — The Holy Bible

We believe the Holy Bible, Old and New Testaments, reveals the Word of God so far as it is necessary for our salvation. It is to be received through the Holy Spirit as the true rule and guide for faith and practice. Whatever is not revealed in or established by the Holy Scriptures is not to be made an article of faith nor is it to be taught as essential to salvation.

THE ARTICLES OF FAITH

5. The Holy Scriptures

We believe that the Holy Scriptures contain everything necessary for salvation. They are to be received through the Holy Spirit as the rule and guide for faith and practice. Whatever is not revealed in or established by the Holy Scriptures is not to be made an article of faith nor is it to be taught as essential to salvation. The Holy Scriptures are those canonical books of the Old and New Testaments which have never been in doubt in the Church. They are the 27 books of the New Testament and the 39 books of the Old Testament.

6. The Old Testament

We believe the Old Testament is not contrary to the New; for everlasting life is offered to humanity in both. Both the Old and New Testaments point to Christ as the only Mediator between God and ourselves. Although the Law given to Moses includes ceremonies, rites, and civil precepts, we are not bound to them. No one, however, is free from obeying the moral commandments.

THE WESLEY QUADRILATERAL

1. Scripture

United Methodists share with other Christians the conviction that Scripture is the primary source and criterion for Christian doctrine. Through Scripture the living Christ meets us in the experience of redeeming grace. We are convinced that Jesus Christ is the living Word of God in our midst whom we trust in life and death.

The biblical authors, illumined by the Holy Spirit, bear witness that in Christ the world is reconciled to God. The Bible bears authentic testimony to God's self-disclosure in the life, death, and resurrection of Jesus Christ as well as in God's work of creation, in the pilgrimage of Israel, and in the Holy Spirit's ongoing activity in human history.

As we open our minds and hearts to the Word of God through the words of human beings inspired by the Holy Spirit, faith is born and nourished, our understanding is deepened, and the possibilities for transforming the world become apparent to us.

The Bible is sacred canon for Christian people, formally acknowledged as such by historic ecumenical councils of the Church. Our doctrinal standards identify as canonical thirty-nine books of the Old Testament and the twenty-seven books of the New Testament.

Our standards affirm the Bible as the source of all that is "necessary" and "sufficient" unto salvation (Articles of Religion) and "is to be received through the Holy Spirit as the true rule and guide for faith and practice" (Confession of Faith).

We properly read Scripture within the believing community, informed by the tradition of that community. We interpret individual texts in light of their place in the Bible as a whole.

We are aided by scholarly inquiry and personal insight, under the guidance of the Holy Spirit. As we work with each text, we take into account what we have been able to learn about the original context and intention of that text. In this understanding we draw upon the careful historical, literary, and textual studies of recent years, which have enriched our understanding of the Bible.

Through this faithful reading of Scripture, we may come to know the truth of the biblical message in its bearing on our own lives and the life of the world. Thus, the Bible serves both as a source of our faith and as the basic criterion by which the truth and fidelity of any interpretation of faith is measured.

While we acknowledge the primacy of Scripture in theological reflection, our attempts to grasp its meaning always involve tradition, experience, and reason. Like Scripture, these may become creative vehicles of the Holy Spirit as they function within the Church. They quicken our faith, open our eyes to the wonder of God's love, and clarify our understanding.

The Wesleyan heritage, reflecting its origins in the catholic and reformed ethos of English Christianity, directs us to a self-conscious use of these three sources in interpreting Scripture and in formulating faith statements based on the biblical witness. These sources are, along with Scripture, indispensable to our theological task.

The close relationship of tradition, experience, and reason appears in the Bible itself. Scripture witnesses to a variety of diverse traditions, some of which reflect tensions in interpretation within the early Judeo-Christian heritage. However, these traditions are woven together in the Bible in a manner that expresses the fundamental unity of God's revelation as received and experienced by people in the diversity of their own lives.

The developing communities of faith judged them, therefore, to be an authoritative witness to that revelation. In recognizing the interrelationship and inseparability of the four basic resources for theological understanding, we are following a model that is present in the biblical text itself.

The United Methodist Discipline

2. Tradition

The theological task does not start anew in each age or each person. Christianity does not leap from New Testament times to the present as though nothing were to be learned from that great cloud of witnesses in between. For centuries Christians have sought to interpret the truth of the gospel for their time.

In these attempts, tradition, understood both in terms of process and form, has played an important role. The passing on and receiving of the gospel among persons, regions, and generations constitutes a dynamic element of Christian history. The formulations and practices that grew out of specific circumstances constitute the legacy of the corporate experience of earlier Christian communities.

These traditions are found in many cultures around the globe. But the history of Christianity includes a mixture of ignorance, misguided zeal, and sin. Scripture remains the norm by which all traditions are judged.

The story of the church reflects the most basic sense of tradition, the continuing activity of God's Spirit transforming human life. Tradition is the history of that continuing environment of grace in and by which all Christians live, God's self-giving love in Jesus Christ. As such, tradition transcends the story of particular traditions.

In this deeper sense of tradition, all Christians share a common history. Within that history, Christian tradition precedes Scripture, and yet Scripture comes to be the focal expression of the tradition. As United Methodists, we pursue our theological task in openness to the richness of both the form and power of tradition.

The multiplicity of traditions furnishes a richly varied source for theological reflection and construction. For United Methodists, certain strands of tradition have special importance as the historic foundation of our doctrinal heritage and the distinctive expressions of our communal existence.

We are now challenged by traditions from around the world that accent dimensions of Christian understanding that grow out of the sufferings and victories of the downtrodden. These traditions help us rediscover the biblical witness to God's special commitment to the poor, the disabled, the imprisoned, the oppressed, the outcast. In these persons we encounter the living presence of Jesus Christ.

These traditions underscore the equality of all persons in Jesus Christ. They display the capacity of the gospel to free us to embrace the diversity of human cultures and appreciate their values. They reinforce our traditional understanding of the inseparability of personal salvation and social justice. They deepen our commitment to global peace.

A critical appreciation of these traditions can compel us to think about God in new ways, enlarge our vision of shalom, and enhance our confidence in God's provident love.

Tradition acts as a measure of validity and propriety for a community's faith insofar as it represents a consensus of faith. The various traditions that presently make claims upon us may contain conflicting images and insights of truth and validity. We examine such conflicts in light of Scripture, reflecting critically upon the doctrinal stance of our Church.

It is by the discerning use of our standards and in openness to emerging forms of Christian identity that we attempt to maintain fidelity to the apostolic faith.

At the same time, we continue to draw on the broader Christian tradition as an expression of the history of divine grace within which Christians are able to recognize and welcome one another in love.

The United Methodist Discipline

VARIATIONS

SCHOOLS OF INTERPRETATION

1. **Fundamentalist** interpreters contribute to our sense of reverence for the Bible. They believe it is the revealed, absolutely perfect, Word of God. They insist that all the words of the Bible are a revelation of God. Therefore they read and study the Bible with complete devotion.

2. **Liberal** interpreters contribute to our appreciation of how, when, and why the Bible was written. They have added to our knowledge of the early scrolls and sources from which our modern versions have come. They insist that the Bible is to be read in historical perspective as an inspired human response to God's revelation.

3. **Neo-Orthodox** interpreters contribute their conviction that we must know what each text and book of the Bible was originally intended to mean before we can know the meaning for our time. They insist that we must not "read into" the Bible our own modern ideas and standards. They want to let the Scriptures speak to us of God's way.

4. **Existential** interpreters contribute to our understanding of how the Bible may speak to our human fears, anxieties, and search for meaning. They believe the Word of God is meant for us as we make decisions about who to be and what to do.

5. **Evangelical** interpreters contribute an appreciation of the Bible as the source of our preaching and living. They insist that the Scriptures call for the conversion of the whole world, until every knee bends and every tongue confesses Jesus Christ as Lord. So they focus our attention upon passages that call for repentance and rebirth as keys to the Christian life.

6. **Charismatic** interpreters contribute their understanding that the Bible can be fully understood or obeyed only by the power of the Holy Spirit in us. They emphasize the role of the Holy Spirit in a living biblical faith. They interpret the Bible in terms of their special experiences of the Holy Spirit.

Mature Christians may learn something from each of these schools of interpretation. All are in agreement of the following basic points: (1) We should love the Bible; (2) We should appreciate how the Scriptures were written and have come to us; (3) We should study the original meaning of

Bible texts; (4) We should let the Word of God speak to our human fears, anxieties, and search for meaning; (5) We should use Scripture as a call for the whole world to believe; and (6) We should be led by the Holy Spirit as we interpret and obey God's Word.

THE THREE MAIN TYPES OF CHRISTIAN MAINSTREAM RELIGION

I. Two questions must be asked:
   A. Is there a God?
   B. Where is God, how can someone get in touch with God?
II. The second question has three answers.
   A. These three answers do not refer to the so called "American" religions: Mormonism, the Seventh Day Adventists, Christian Scientists, New Age practioners, Jehovah's Witnesses, etc.
   B. The different answers are primarily a difference in emphasis.

THE BIBLICAL ANSWER	THE PERSONAL WITNESS ANSWER	THE SACRAMENTAL ANSWER
Lutherans Some Fundamentalists Methodists Presbyterians United Church of Christ Some Baptist Groups	Billy Graham Jerry Falwell The "700 Club" Some Baptist Groups Most "Born Again" Groups Assemblies of God Pentecostal Churches	Roman Catholics Anglicans and Episcopalians All Eastern Christian Churches (Such as Greek Orthodox, etc.)
THE WORSHIP FOCUS OF THESE THREE GROUPS		
Preaching on the Bible	Preaching on the Bible AND giving personal witness to one's relationship with Christ	The sacraments and scripture as included in the sacraments
THE PERSONAL PRACTICES OF THESE THREE TYPES		
Learning the Bible and doing what it says as interpreted by the Church	Having a personal, transforming and ongoing relationship with Christ and sharing the experience with others for their salvation	Participating in the sacramental life of the Church
THE THEOLOGICAL THRUST OF THESE THREE GROUPS		
Prophetic	Ecstatic	Cultic

III. All three require intense personal commitment and dedication to community life. Some are better at both of these than others.
   A. A difficult area for many of these religious groups is attention to the poor.
   B. Almost all groups sponsor some form of missionary activity.
   C. Roman Catholics and Fundamentalist membership is on the rise in the U.S.
   D. Mainline Protestant denominations are in decline regarding membership.

Presented for the Wisconsin Council of Catholic Women in Waupun, on Thursday, May 8, 1997 by Father Ken Omernck

7. SIN AND SALVATION

The Methodist Articles of Religion

VII through XII

The Evangelical United Brethren Confession of Faith

VII through XII

The Articles of Faith

7 through 12 and 27

The Wesley Quadrilateral

Experience and Reason

Wesley's Sermon

The Scripture Way of Salvation

THE METHODIST ARTICLES OF RELIGION

Article VII—Of Original or Birth Sin

Original sin standeth not in the following of Adam (as the Pelagians do vainly talk), but it is the corruption of the nature of every man, that naturally is engendered of the offspring of Adam, whereby man is very far gone from original righteousness, and of his own nature inclined to evil, and that continually.

Article VIII—Of Free Will

The condition of man after the fall of Adam is such that he cannot turn and prepare himself, by his own natural strength and works, to faith, and calling upon God; wherefore we have no power to do good works, pleasant and acceptable to God, without the grace of God by Christ preventing us, that we may have a good will, and working with us, when we have that good will.

Article IX—Of the Justification of Man

We are accounted righteous before God only for the merit of our Lord and Saviour Jesus Christ, by faith, and not for our own works or deservings. Wherefore, that we are justified by faith, only, is a most wholesome doctrine, and very full of comfort.

Article X—Of Good Works

Although good works, which are the fruits of faith, and follow after justification, cannot put away our sins, and endure the severity of God's judgment; yet are they pleasing and acceptable to God in Christ, and spring out of a true and lively faith, insomuch that by them a lively faith may be as evidently known as a tree is discerned by its fruit.

Article XI—Of Works of Supererogation

Voluntary works—besides, over and above God's commandments—which they call works of supererogation, cannot be taught without arrogancy and impiety. For by them men do declare that they do not only render unto God as much as they are bound to do, but that they do more for his sake than of bounden duty is required; whereas Christ saith plainly: When you have done all that is commanded you, say, We are unprofitable servants.

Article XII — Of Sin After Justification

Not every sin willingly committed after justification is the sin against the Holy Ghost, and unpardonable. Wherefore, the grant of repentance is not to be denied to such as fall into sin after justification. After we have received the Holy Ghost, we may depart from grace given, and fall into sin, and, by the grace of God, rise again and amend our lives. And therefore they are to be condemned who say they can no more sin as long as they live here; or deny the place of forgiveness to such as truly repent.

Of Sanctification

[The following Article from the Methodist Protestant Discipline is placed here by the Uniting Conference (1939). It was not one of the Articles of Religion voted upon by the three churches.]

Sanctification is that renewal of our fallen nature by the Holy Ghost, received through faith in Jesus Christ, whose blood of atonement cleanseth from all sin; whereby we are not only delivered from the guilt of sin, but are washed from its pollution, saved from its power, and are enabled, through grace, to love God with all our hearts and to walk in his holy commandments blameless.

THE EVANGELICAL UNITED BRETHREN CONFESSION OF FAITH

Article VII — Sin and Free Will

We believe man is fallen from righteousness and, apart from the grace of our Lord Jesus Christ, is destitute of holiness and inclined to evil. Except a man be born again, he cannot see the Kingdom of God. In his own strength, without divine grace, man cannot do good works pleasing and acceptable to God. We believe, however, man influenced and empowered by the Holy Spirit is responsible in freedom to exercise his will for good.

Article VIII — Reconciliation Through Christ

We believe God was in Christ reconciling the world to himself. The offering Christ freely made on the cross is the perfect and sufficient sacrifice for the sins of the whole world, redeeming man from all sin, so that no other satisfaction is required.

Article IX—Justification and Regeneration

We believe we are never accounted righteous before God through our works or merit, but that penitent sinners are justified or accounted righteous before God only by faith in our Lord Jesus Christ.

We believe regeneration is the renewal of man in righteousness through Jesus Christ, by the power of the Holy Spirit, whereby we are made partakers of the divine nature and experience newness of life. By this new birth the believer becomes reconciled to God and is enabled to serve him with the will and the affections.

We believe, although we have experienced regeneration, it is possible to depart from grace and fall into sin; and we may even then, by the grace of God, be renewed in righteousness.

Article X—Good Works

We believe good works are the necessary fruits of faith and follow regeneration but they do not have the virtue to remove our sins or to avert divine judgment. We believe good works, pleasing and acceptable to God in Christ, spring from a true and living faith, for through and by them faith is made evident.

Article XI—Sanctification and Christian Perfection

We believe sanctification is the work of God's grace through the Word and the Spirit, by which those who have been born again are cleansed from sin in their thoughts, words and acts, and are enabled to live in accordance with God's will, and to strive for holiness without which no one will see the Lord.

Entire sanctification is a state of perfect love, righteousness and true holiness which every regenerate believer may obtain by being delivered from the power of sin, by loving God with all the heart, soul, mind and strength, and by loving one's neighbor as one's self. Through faith in Jesus Christ this gracious gift may be received in this life both gradually and instantaneously, and should be sought earnestly by every child of God.

We believe this experience does not deliver us from the infirmities, ignorance, and mistakes common to man, nor from the possibilities of further sin. The Christian must continue on guard against spiritual pride and seek to gain victory over every temptation to sin. He must respond wholly to the will of God so that sin will lose its power over him; and the world, the flesh, and the devil are put under his feet. Thus he rules over these enemies with watchfulness through the power of the Holy Spirit.

Article XII — The Judgment and the Future State

We believe all men stand under the righteous judgment of Jesus Christ, both now and in the last day. We believe in the resurrection of the dead; the righteous to life eternal and the wicked to endless condemnation.

THE ARTICLES OF FAITH

7. Sin

We believe all of us, like Adam, possess a corrupted nature. In this state we are inclined towards evil and unable to recover the original righteousness for which we were created.

8. Free Will

We believe that in our own strength, without the help of divine grace, we are unable to do good works that are pleasing and acceptable to God; but when we are influenced and empowered by the Holy Spirit, we are set free and become responsible to exercise his will for good.

9. Justification by Grace Alone

We believe that it is only on the merit of our Lord and Savior Jesus Christ that God accepts us as righteous. We are never accepted as righteous before God on the basis of our own good works. Justification before God comes by grace alone and our response to it in faith.

10. Good Works

We believe that although good works cannot remove our sins so that we can escape judgment, they are the fruit of faith which follow our justification before God. They are pleasing and acceptable to God and spring from a true and living faith in Christ.

11. Works of Supererogation

We believe that voluntary works, over and above God's commandments, are called works of supererogation; and they cannot be taught without arrogance and self-righteousness. Those who think that they have done more than their duty are mistaken, for Christ has plainly taught: "...when you have done all you have been told to do, say, 'We are ordinary servants; we have only done our duty.'" (Luke 17:10)

12. Sin After Justification

We believe that after we have received the Holy Spirit, it is possible for us to fall into sin, but not every sin voluntarily committed after justification is an unpardonable sin against the Holy Spirit. While we can fall into sin after we have once known the grace of God, forgiveness is still available for all who truly repent and by the grace of God rise again and change their lives.

27. Sanctification and Christian Perfection

We believe Sanctification is the work of God's grace on us which cleanses us from sin in our thoughts, words, and deeds, and enables us to live in accordance with God's Will. Entire sanctification is a state of perfect love in which we are given the power to love God with all our heart, soul, mind, and strength, and to love our neighbor as we love ourselves. Through faith in Jesus Christ this gift may be received gradually or instantaneously, but should be earnestly sought by all. This experience does not deliver us from the infirmities, ignorance, and mistakes common to humanity, nor does it mean that we will no longer sin. As Christians we must continue to guard against spiritual pride, but we must also seek to gain victory over every temptation. We must respond wholly to the Will of God.

THE WESLEY QUADRILATERAL

3. Reason

Although we recognize that God's revelation and our experiences of God's grace continually surpass the scope of human language and reason, we also believe that any disciplined theological work calls for the careful use of reason.

By reason we read and interpret Scripture.

By reason we determine whether our Christian witness is clear.

By reason we ask questions of faith and seek to understand God's action and will.

By reason we organize the understandings that compose our witness and render them internally coherent.

By reason we test the congruence of our witness to the biblical testimony and to the traditions that mediate that testimony to us.

By reason we relate our witness to the full range of human knowledge, experience, and service.

Since all truth is from God, efforts to discern the connections between revelation and reason, faith and science, grace and nature, are useful endeavors in developing credible and communicable doctrine. We seek nothing less than a total view of reality that is decisively informed by the promises and imperatives of the Christian gospel, though we know well that such an attempt will always be marred by the limits and distortions characteristic of human knowledge.

Nevertheless, by our quest for reasoned understandings of Christian faith we seek to grasp, express, and live out the gospel in a way that will commend itself to thoughtful persons who are seeking to know and follow God's ways.

In theological reflection, the resources of tradition, experience, and reason are integral to our study of Scripture without displacing Scripture's primacy for faith and practice. These four sources—each making distinctive contributions, yet all finally working together—guide our quest as United Methodists for a vital and appropriate Christian witness.

The United Methodist Discipline

4. Experience

In our theological task, we follow Wesley's practice of examining experience, both individual and corporate, for confirmations of the realities of God's grace attested in Scripture.

Our experience interacts with Scripture. We read Scripture in light of the conditions and events that help shape who we are, and we interpret our experience in terms of Scripture.

All religious experience affects all human experience; all human experience affects our understanding of religious experience.

On the personal level, experience is to the individual as tradition is to the church: It is the personal appropriation of God's forgiving and empowering grace. Experience authenticates in our own lives the truths revealed in Scripture and illumined in tradition, enabling us to claim the Christian witness as our own.

Wesley described faith and its assurance as "a sure trust and confidence" in the mercy of God through our Lord Jesus Christ, and a steadfast hope of all good things to be received at God's hand. Such assurance is God's gracious gift through the witness of the Holy Spirit.

This "new life in Christ" is what we as United Methodists mean when we speak of "Christian experience." Christian experience gives us new eyes to see the living truth in Scripture. It confirms the biblical message for our present. It illumines our understanding of God and creation and motivates us to make sensitive moral judgments.

Although profoundly personal, Christian experience is also corporate; our theological task is informed by the experience of the church and by the common experiences of all humanity. In our attempts to understand the biblical message, we recognize that God's gift of liberating love embraces the whole of creation.

Some facets of human experience tax our theological understanding. Many of God's people live in terror, hunger, loneliness, and degradation. Everyday experiences of birth and death, of growth and life in the created world, and an awareness of wider social relations also belong to serious theological reflection.

A new awareness of such experiences can inform our appropriation of scriptural truths and sharpen our appreciation of the good news of the kingdom of God.

As a source for theological reflection, experience, like tradition, is richly varied, challenging our efforts to put into words the totality of the promises of the gospel. We interpret experience in the light of scriptural norms, just as our experience informs our reading of the biblical message. In this respect, Scripture remains central in our efforts to be faithful in making our Christian witness.

The United Methodist Discipline

THE SCRIPTURE WAY OF SALVATION

"Ye are saved through faith."
Ephesians ii. 8.

1. NOTHING can be more intricate, complex, and hard to be understood than religion, as it has been often described. And this is not only true concerning the religion of the Heathens, even many of the wisest of them, but concerning the religion of those also who were, in some sense, Christians; yea, and men of great name in the Christian world; men who seemed to be pillars thereof. Yet how easy to be understood, how plain and simple a thing is the genuine religion of Jesus Christ; provided only that we take it in its native form, just as it is described in the oracles of God! It is exactly suited, by the wise Creator and Governor of the world, to the weak understanding and narrow capacity of man in his present state. How observable is this, both with regard to the end it proposes, and the means to attain that end! The end is, in one word, salvation; the means to attain it, faith.

2. It is easily discerned, that these two little words, I mean faith and salvation, include the substance of all the Bible, the marrow, as it were, of the whole Scripture. So much the more should we take all possible care to avoid all mistake concerning them, and to form a true and accurate judgment concerning both the one and the other.

3. Let us then seriously inquire,

I. What is salvation?

II. What is that faith whereby we are saved? And,

III. How we are saved by it?

1. And, First, let us inquire, What is salvation? The salvation which is here spoken of is not what is frequently understood by that word, the going to heaven, eternal happiness. It is not the soul's going to paradise, termed by our Lord, "Abraham's bosom." It is not a blessing which lies on the other side death; or, as we usually speak, in the oilier world. The very words of the text itself put this beyond all question: "Ye are saved." It is not something at a distance: It is a present thing; a blessing which, through the free mercy of God, ye are now in possession of. Nay, the words may be rendered, and that with equal propriety, "Ye have been saved:" So that the salvation which is here spoken of might be extended to the entire work of God, from the first dawning of grace in the soul, till it is consummated in glory.

2. If we take this in its utmost extent, it will include all that is wrought in the soul by what is frequently termed natural conscience, but more properly, preventing grace; — all the drawings of the Father; the desires after God, which, if we yield to them, increase more and more; — all that light wherewith the Son of God "enlighteneth every one that cometh into the world;" showing every man "to do justly, to love mercy, and to walk humbly with his God;" — all the convictions which his Spirit, from time to time, works in every child of man; although, it is true, the generality of men stifle them as soon as possible, and after a while forget, or at least deny, that they ever had them at all.

3. But we are at present concerned only with that salvation which the Apostle is directly speaking of. And this consists of two general parts, justification and sanctification.

Justification is another word for pardon. It is the forgiveness of all our sins; and, what is necessarily implied therein, our acceptance with God. The price whereby this hath been procured for us, (commonly termed the meritorious cause of our justification,) is the blood and righteousness of Christ; or, to express it a little more clearly, all that Christ hath done and suffered for us, till he "poured out his soul for the transgressors."

The immediate effects of justification are, the peace of God, a "peace that passeth all understanding," and a "rejoicing in hope of the glory of God" "with joy unspeakable and full of glory."

4. And at the same time that we are justified, yea, in that very moment, sanctification begins. In that instant we are born again, born from above, born of the Spirit: There is a real as well as a relative change. We are inwardly renewed by the power of God. We feel "the love of God shed abroad in our heart by the Holy Ghost which is given unto us;" producing love to all mankind, and more especially to the children of God; expelling the love of the world, the love of pleasure, of ease, of honour, of money, together with pride, anger, self-will, and every other evil temper; in a word, changing the earthly, sensual, devilish mind, into "the mind which was in Christ Jesus."

5. How naturally do those who experience such a change imagine that all sin is gone; that it is utterly rooted out of their heart, and has no more any place therein! How easily do they draw that inference, "I feel no sin; therefore, I have none: It does not stir; therefore, it does not exist: It has no motion; therefore, it has no being!"

6. But it is seldom long before they are undeceived, finding sin was only suspended, not destroyed. Temptations return, and sin revives; showing it was but stunned before, not dead. They now feel two principles in

themselves, plainly contrary to each other; "the flesh lusting against the Spirit;" nature opposing the grace of God. They cannot deny, that, although they still feel power to believe in Christ, and to love God; and although his "Spirit" still "witnesses with their spirits, that they are children of God;" yet they feel in themselves sometimes pride or self-will, sometimes anger or unbelief. They find one or more of these frequently stirring in their heart, though not conquering; yea, perhaps, "thrusting sore at them that they may fall;" but the Lord is their help.

7. How exactly did Macarius, fourteen hundred years ago, describe the present experience of the children of God! "The unskilful," or unexperienced, "when grace operates, presently imagine they have no more sin. Whereas they that have discretion cannot deny, that even we who have the grace of God may be molested again. — For we have often had instances of some among the brethren, who have experienced such grace as to affirm that they had no sin in them; and yet, after all, when they thought themselves entirely freed from it, the corruption that lurked within was stirred up anew, and they were well nigh burned up."

8. From the time of our being born again, the gradual work of sanctification takes place. We are enabled "by the Spirit" to "mortify the deeds of the body," of our evil nature; and as we are more and more dead to sin, we are more and more alive to God. We go on from grace to grace, while we are careful to "abstain from all appearance of evil," and are "zealous of good works," as we have opportunity, doing good to all men; while we walk in all His ordinances blameless, therein worshiping Him in spirit and in truth; while we take up our cross, and deny ourselves every pleasure that does not lead us to God.

9. It is thus that we wait for entire sanctification; for a full salvation from all our sins, — from pride, self-will, anger, unbelief; or, as the Apostle expresses it, "go on unto perfection." But what is perfection? The word has various senses: Here it means perfect love. It is love excluding sin; love filling the heart, taking up the whole capacity of the soul. It is love "rejoicing evermore, praying without ceasing, in every thing giving thanks."

II. But what is that faith through which we are saved? This is the Second point to be considered.

1. Faith, in general, is defined by the Apostle, pragmaton elegchos ou blepomenon - An evidence, A divine evidence and conviction (the word means both) of things not seen; not visible, not perceivable either by sight, or by any other of the external senses. It implies both a supernatural evidence of God, and of the things of God; a kind of spiritual light

exhibited to the soul, and a supernatural sight or perception thereof. Accordingly, the Scripture speaks of God's giving sometimes light, sometimes a power of discerning it. So St. Paul: "God, who commanded light to shine out of darkness, hath shined in our hearts, to give us the light of the knowledge of the glory of God in the face of Jesus Christ." And else where the same Apostle speaks of "the eyes of" our "understanding being opened." By this two-fold operation of the Holy Spirit, having the eyes of our soul both opened and enlightened we see the things which the natural "eye hath not seen, neither the ear heard." We have a prospect of the invisible things of God; we see the spiritual world, which is all round about us, and yet no more discerned by our natural faculties than if it had no being: And we see the eternal world; piercing through the veil which hangs between time and eternity. Clouds and darkness then rest upon it no more, but we already see the glory which shall be revealed.

2. Taking the word in a more particular sense, faith is a divine evidence and conviction, not only that "God was in Christ, reconciling the world unto himself," but also that Christ loved me, and gave himself for me. It is by this faith (whether we term it the essence, or rather a property thereof) that we receive Christ; that we receive him in all his offices, as our Prophet, Priest, and King. It is by this that he is "made of God unto us wisdom, and righteousness, and sanctification, and redemption."

3. "But is this the faith of assurance, or faith of adherence?" The Scripture mentions no such distinction. The Apostle says, "There is one faith, and one hope of our calling;" one Christian, saving faith; "as there is one Lord," in whom we believe, and "one God and Father of us all." And it is certain, this faith necessarily implies an assurance (which is here only another word for evidence, it being hard to tell the difference between them) that Christ loved me, and gave himself for me. For "he that believeth" with the true living faith, "hath the witness in himself:" "The Spirit witnesseth with his spirit, that he is a child of God." "Because he is a son, God hath sent forth the Spirit of his Son into his heart, crying, Abba, Father;" giving him an assurance that he is so, and a childlike confidence in him. But let it be observed, that, in the very nature of the thing, the assurance goes before the confidence. For a man cannot have a childlike confidence in God till he knows he is a child of God. Therefore confidence, trust, reliance, adherence, or whatever else it be called, is not the first, as some have supposed, but the second branch or act of faith.

4. It is by this faith we are saved, justified and sanctified; taking that word in its highest sense. But how are we justified and sanctified by faith? This is our Third head of inquiry. And this being the main point in question, and

a point of no ordinary importance, it will not be improper to give it a more distinct and particular consideration.

III. 1. And, First, how are we justified by faith? In what sense is this to be understood? I answer, Faith is the condition, and the only condition, of justification. It is the condition: None is justified but he that believes: Without faith no man is justified. And it is the only condition: This alone is sufficient for justification. Every one that believes is justified, whatever else he has or has not. In other words: No man is justified till he believes; every man, when he believes, is justified.

2. "But does not God command us to repent also? Yea, and to 'bring forth fruits meet for repentance?' — to cease, for instance, from doing evil; and learn to do well? And is not both the one and the other of the utmost necessity, insomuch that if we willingly neglect either, we cannot reasonably expect to be justified at all? But if this be so, how can it be said that faith is the only condition of justification?"

God does undoubtedly command us both to repent, and to bring forth fruits meet for repentance; which if we willingly neglect, we cannot reasonably expect to be justified at all: Therefore both repentance, and fruits meet for repentance, are, in some sense, necessary to justification. But they are not necessary in the same sense with faith, nor in the same degree. Not in the same degree; for those fruits are only necessary conditionally; if there be time and opportunity for them. Otherwise a man may be justified without them, as was the thief upon the cross; (if we may call him so; for a late writer has discovered that he was no thief, but a very honest and respectable person!) but he cannot be justified without faith; this is impossible. Likewise, let a man have ever so much repentance, or ever so many of the fruits meet for repentance, yet all this does not at all avail; he is not justified till he believes. But the moment he believes, with or without those fruits, yea, with more or less repentance, he is justified. — Not in the same sense; for repentance and its fruits are only remotely necessary; necessary in order to faith; whereas faith is immediately and directly necessary to justification. It remains, that faith is the only condition, which is immediately and proximately necessary to justification.

3. "But do you believe we are sanctified by faith? We know you believe that we are justified by faith; but do not you believe, and accordingly teach, that we are sanctified by our works?" So it has been roundly and vehemently affirmed for these five-and-twenty years: But I have constantly declared just the contrary; and that in all manner of ways. I have continually testified in private and in public, that we are sanctified as well as justified by faith. And indeed the one of those great truths does exceedingly illustrate the other. Exactly as we are justified by faith, so are

we sanctified by faith. Faith is the condition, and the only condition, of sanctification, exactly as it is of justification. It is the condition: None is sanctified but he that believes; without faith no man is sanctified. And it is the only condition: This alone is sufficient for sanctification. Every one that believes is sanctified, whatever else he has or has not. In other words, no man is sanctified till he believes: Every man when he believes is sanctified.

4. "But is there not a repentance consequent upon, as well as a repentance previous to, justification? And is it not incumbent on all that are justified to be 'zealous of good works?' Yea, are not these so necessary, that if a man willingly neglect them he cannot reasonably expect that he shall ever be sanctified in the full sense; that is, perfected in love? Nay, can he grow at all in grace, in the loving knowledge of our Lord Jesus Christ? Yea, can he retain the grace which God has already given him? Can he continue in the faith which he has received, or in the favour of God? Do not you yourself allow all this, and continually assert it? But, if this be so, how can it be said that faith is the only condition of sanctification?"

5. I do allow all this, and continually maintain it as the truth of God. I allow there is a repentance consequent upon, as well as a repentance previous to, justification. It is incumbent on all that are justified to be zealous of good works. And these are so necessary, that if a man willingly neglect them, he cannot reasonably expect that he shall ever be sanctified; he cannot grow in grace, in the image of God, the mind which was in Christ Jesus; nay, he cannot retain the grace he has received; he cannot continue in faith, or in the favour of God.

What is the inference we must draw herefrom? Why, that both repentance, rightly understood, and the practice of all good works, — works of piety, as well as works of mercy, (now properly so called, since they spring from faith,) are, in some sense, necessary to sanctification.

6. I say, repentance rightly understood; for this must not be confounded with the former repentance. The repentance consequent upon justification is widely different from that which is antecedent to it. This implies no guilt, no sense of condemnation, no consciousness of the wrath of God. It does not suppose any doubt of the favour of God, or any "fear that hath torment." It is properly a conviction, wrought by the Holy Ghost, of the sin which still remains in our heart; of the phronema sarkos, the carnal mind, which "does still remain," (as our Church speaks,) "even in them that are regenerate;" although it does no longer reign; it has not now dominion over them. It is a conviction of our proneness to evil, of an heart bent to backsliding, of the still continuing tendency of the flesh to lust against the spirit. Sometimes, unless we continually watch and pray, it lusteth to pride, sometimes to anger, sometimes to love of the world, love of ease, love of

honour, or love of pleasure more than of God. It is a conviction of the tendency of our heart to self-will, to Atheism, or idolatry; and, above all, to unbelief, whereby, in a thousand ways, and under a thousand pretences, we are ever departing, more or less, from the living God.

7. With this conviction of the sin remaining in our hearts, there is joined a clear conviction of the sin remaining in our lives; still cleaving to all our words and actions. In the best of these we now discern a mixture of evil, either in the spirit, the matter, or the manner of them; something that could not endure the righteous judgment of God, were he extreme to mark what is done amiss. Where we least suspected it, we find a taint of pride, or self-will, of unbelief, or idolatry; so that we are now more ashamed of our best duties than formerly of our worst sins: And hence we cannot but feel that these are so far from having any thing meritorious in them, yea, so far from being able to stand in sight of the divine justice, that for those also we should be guilty before God, were it not for the blood of the covenant.

8. Experience shows that, together with this conviction of sin remaining in our hearts, and cleaving to all our words and actions; as well as the guilt which on account thereof we should incur, were we not continually sprinkled with the atoning blood; one thing more is implied in this repentance; namely, a conviction of our helplessness, of our utter inability to think one good thought, or to form one good desire; and much more to speak one word aright, or to perform one good action, but through his free almighty grace, first preventing us, and then accompanying us every moment.

9. "But what good works are those, the practice of which you affirm to be necessary to sanctification?" First, all works of piety; such as public prayer, family prayer, and praying in our closet; receiving the supper of the Lord; searching the Scriptures, by hearing, reading, meditating; and using such a measure of fasting or abstinence as our bodily health allows.

10. Secondly, all works of mercy; whether they relate to the bodies or souls of men; such as feeding the hungry, clothing the naked, entertaining the stranger, visiting those that are in prison, or sick, or variously afflicted; such as the endeavouring to instruct the ignorant, to awaken the stupid sinner, to quicken the lukewarm, to confirm the wavering, to comfort the feebleminded, to succour the tempted, or contribute in any manner to the saving of souls from death. This is the repentance, and these the "fruits meet for repentance," which are necessary to full sanctification. This is the way wherein God hath appointed his children to wait for complete salvation.

11. Hence may appear the extreme mischievousness of that seemingly innocent opinion, that there is no sin in a believer; that all sin is destroyed, root and branch, the moment a man is justified. By totally preventing that repentance, it quite blocks up the way to sanctification. There is no place for repentance in him who believes there is no sin either in his life or heart: Consequently, there is no place for his being perfected in love, to which that repentance is indispensably necessary.

12. Hence it may likewise appear, that there is no possible danger in thus expecting full salvation. For suppose we were mistaken, suppose no such blessing ever was or can be attained, yet we lose nothing: Nay, that very expectation quickens us in using all the talents which God has given us; yea, in improving them all; so that when our Lord cometh, he will receive his own with increase.

13. But to return. Though it be allowed, that both this repentance and its fruits are necessary to full salvation; yet they are not necessary either in the same sense with faith, or in the same degree: — Not in the same degree; for these fruits are only necessary conditionally, if there be time and opportunity for them; otherwise a man may be sanctified without them. But he cannot be sanctified without faith. Likewise, let a man have ever so much of this repentance, or ever so many good works, yet all this does not at all avail: He is not sanctified till he believes. But the moment he believes, with or without those fruits, yea, with more or less of this repentance, he is sanctified. — Not in the same sense; for this repentance and these fruits are only remotely necessary, — necessary in order to the continuance of his faith, as well as the increase of it; whereas faith is immediately and directly necessary to sanctification. It remains, that faith is the only condition which is immediately and proximately necessary to sanctification.

14. "But what is that faith whereby we are sanctified; — saved from sin, and perfected in love?" It is a divine evidence and conviction, First, that God hath promised it in the Holy Scripture. Till we are thoroughly satisfied of this, there is no moving one step further. And one would imagine there needed not one word more to satisfy a reasonable man of this, than the ancient promise, "Then will I circumcise thy heart, and the heart of thy seed, to love the Lord thy God with all thy heart, and with all thy soul, and with all thy mind." How clearly does this express the being perfected in love! — how strongly imply the being saved from all sin! For as long as love takes up the whole heart, what room is there for sin therein?

15. It is a divine evidence and conviction, Secondly, that what God hath promised he is able to perform. Admitting, therefore, that "with men it is impossible" to "bring a clean thing out of an unclean," to purify the heart from all sin, and to fill it with all holiness; yet this creates no difficulty in the case, seeing "with God all things are possible." And surely no one ever imagined it was possible to any power less than that of the Almighty! But if God speaks, it shall be done. God saith, "Let there be light; and there" is "light!"

16. It is, Thirdly, a divine evidence and Conviction that he is able and willing to do it now. And why not? Is not a moment to him the same as a thousand years? He cannot want more time to accomplish whatever is his will. And he cannot want or stay for any more worthiness or fitness in the persons he is pleased to honour. We may therefore boldly say, at any point of time, "Now is the day of salvation!" "To-day, if ye will hear his voice, harden not your hearts!" "Behold, all things are now ready; come unto the marriage!"

17. To this confidence, that God is both able and willing to sanctify us now, there needs to be added one thing more, — a divine evidence and conviction that he doeth it. In that hour it is done: God says to the inmost soul, "According to thy faith be it unto thee!" Then the soul is pure from every spot of sin; it is clean "from all unrighteousness." The believer then experiences the deep meaning of those solemn words, "If we walk in the light as He is in the light, we have fellowship one with another, and the blood of Jesus Christ his Son cleanseth us from all sin."

18. "But does God work this great work in the soul gradually or instantaneously?" Perhaps it may be gradually wrought in some; I mean in this sense, they do not advert to the particular moment wherein sin ceases to be. But it is infinitely desirable, were it the will of God, that it should be done instantaneously; that the Lord should destroy sin "by the breath of his mouth," in a moment, in the twinkling of an eye. And so he generally does; a plain fact, of which there is evidence enough to satisfy any unprejudiced person. Thou therefore look for it every moment! Look for it in the way above described; in all those good works whereunto thou art "created anew in Christ Jesus." There is then no danger: You can be no worse, if you are no better, for that expectation. For were you to be disappointed of your hope, still you lose nothing. But you shall not be disappointed of your hope: It will come, and will not tarry. Look for it then every day, every hour, every moment! Why not this hour, this moment? Certainly you may look for it now, if you believe it is by faith. And by this token you may surely know whether you seek it by faith or by works. If by works, you want something to be done first, before you are sanctified. You think, I

must first be or do thus or thus. Then you are seeking it by works unto this day. If you seek it by faith, you may expect it as you are; and if as you are, then expect it now. It is of importance to observe, that there is an inseparable connexion between these three points, — expect it by faith, expect it as you are, and expect it now! To deny one of them, is to deny them all; to allow one, is to allow them all. Do you believe we are sanctified by faith? Be true then to your principle; and look for this blessing just as you are, neither better nor worse; as a poor sinner that has still nothing to pay, nothing to plead, but "Christ died." And if you look for it as you are, then expect it now. Stay for nothing: Why should you? Christ is ready; and He is all you want. He is waiting for you: He is at the door! Let your inmost soul cry out,

Come in, come in, thou heavenly Guest!
Nor hence again remove;
But sup with me, and let the feast
Be everlasting love.

SCRIPTURE WAY OF SALVATION OUTLINE

"For it is by grace you have been saved, through faith."

Ephesians 2:8

Salvation is Simple.

"...how easy to be understood, how plain and simple a thing is the genuine religion of Jesus Christ; provided only that we take it in its native form, just as it is described in the oracles [word] of God!"

1. WHAT IS SALVATION

"The salvation which is here spoken of is not what is frequently understood by that word, the going to heaven, eternal happiness. ... It is not a blessing which lies on the other side [of] death...."

"The very words of the text itself put this beyond all question: 'Ye are saved.' It is not something at a distance: It is a present thing; a blessing...."

"[Salvation] consists of two general parts, **justification** and **Sanctification**."

"Justification is another word for pardon. It is forgiveness of all our sins...."

"The immediate effects of justification are, the peace of God, a 'peace that passeth all understanding,' and a 'rejoicing in hope of the glory of God' 'with joy unspeakable and full of glory.'"

"And at the same time that we are justified, yea, in that very moment, sanctification begins."

"'The unskillful,' or unexperienced, 'when grace operates, presently imagine they have no more sin.'"

"...we wait for entire sanctification; for a full salvation from all our sins,—from pride, self-will, anger, unbelief; or, as the Apostle expresses it, "go on unto perfection."

"But what is perfection? The word has various senses: Here it means perfect love. It is love excluding sin; love filling the heart, taking up the whole capacity of the soul."

2. WHAT IS FAITH?

"[Faith is] A divine **evidence** and **conviction**...of things not seen...a kind of spiritual light exhibited to the soul."

"By this two-fold operation of the Holy Spirit, having the eyes of our soul both opened and enlightened we see the things which the natural "eye hath not seen, neither the ear heard.""

"...faith is a divine evidence and conviction not only that 'God was in Christ, reconciling the world unto himself,' but also that Christ loved me, and gave himself for me."

Assurance. "For a man cannot have a childlike confidence in God till he knows he is a child of God."

Adherence. "...adherence...is not the first, as some have supposed, but the second branch or act of faith."

3. HOW ARE WE SAVED?

"Faith is the condition, and the only condition, of justification. ... Every one that believes is justified.... No man is justified till he believes; every man, when he believes is justified."

What about **repentance** and **fruits** (good works)? "God does undoubtedly command us both to repent, and to bring forth fruits...." "....those fruits are only necessary conditionally; if there be time and opportunity for them. Otherwise a man may be justified without them, as was the thief upon the cross."

"...we are sanctified as well as justified by faith." "Every one that believes is sanctified...no man is sanctified till he believes: Every man when he believes is sanctified."

"...works of piety, as well as works of mercy (springing from faith) are, in some sense, necessary to sanctification."

Works of Piety: "First, all works of piety; such as public prayer, family prayer, and praying in our closet; receiving the supper of the Lord; searching the Scriptures, by hearing, reading, meditation; and using such a measure of fasting or abstinence as our bodily health allows."

Works of Mercy: "...such as feeding the hungry, clothing the naked, entertaining the stranger, visiting those that are in prison, or sick, or variously afflicted...."

"...repentance and its fruits are necessary to full salvation...." "

We are "saved from sin, and perfected in love." "But does God work this great work in the soul gradually or instantaneously? Perhaps it may be gradually wrought in some; I mean in this sense, they do not advert to the particular moment wherein sin ceases to be. But it is infinitely desirable, were it the will of God, that it should be done instantaneously...."

"It is of importance to observe, that there is an inseparable connexion between these three points, —expect it by faith, expect it as you are, and expect it now!

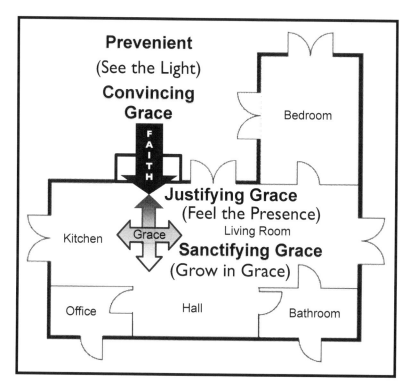

THREE KINDS OF GRACE

John Wesley compares salvation and God's grace to a house.

1. Prevenient grace means "going before." Like being on the front porch of a house. Through prevenient grace, God seeks us and invites us into a relationship, but we haven't yet accepted the invitation.

2. Justifying grace is like entering the front door of a house. When we respond to God's invitation and open the door into God's house, we are right with God and have assurance that our sins are forgiven. God pardons our sins and assures us that we are right with God. Some people call this moment "being saved."

3. Sanctifying grace is when we enter the house. Once we're in the house, there are a lot rooms to explore. This enables us to mature in faith, become more like Christ, and become the people God desires us to be.

THE TEMPLE OF GOD

*Surely you know that you're God's Temple
and that God's Spirit lives in you!*

1 Corinthians 3:16

Imagine yourself as a living house.
God comes in to rebuild that house.

At first, perhaps, you can understand what He is doing. He is getting the drains right and stopping the leaks in the roof and so on: you knew that those jobs needed doing and so you are not surprised. But presently he starts knocking the house about in a way that hurts abominably and does not seem to make sense.

What on earth is He up to?

The explanation is that He is building quite a different house from the one you thought of—throwing out a new wing here, putting on an extra floor there, running up towers, making courtyards.

You thought you were going to be made into a decent little cottage: but He is building a palace.

He intends to come live in it Himself.

George MacDonald[1]

---

[1] Quoted from C.S. Lewis, *Mere Christianity* (New York: Touchstone, 1980), p. 176.

8. CHURCH AND SACRAMENTS

The Methodist Articles of Religion

XIII through XXII (and XXVI)

The Evangelical United Brethren Confession of Faith

V through VII and XIII through XIV

The Articles of Faith

13 through 22 and 26

The Christian Year

Advent
Christmas
Epiphany
Lent
Easter
Pentecost
Trinity Sunday

THE METHODIST ARTICLES OF RELIGION

Article XIII—Of the Church

The visible church of Christ is a congregation of faithful men in which the pure Word of God is preached, and the Sacraments duly administered according to Christ's ordinance, in all those things that of necessity are requisite to the same.

Article XIV—Of Purgatory

The Romish doctrine concerning purgatory, pardon, worshiping, and adoration, as well of images as of relics, and also invocation of saints, is a fond thing, vainly invented, and grounded upon no warrant of Scripture, but repugnant to the Word of God.

Article XV—Of Speaking in the Congregation in Such a Tongue
as the People Understand

It is a thing plainly repugnant to the Word of God, and the custom of the primitive church, to have public prayer in the church, or to minister the Sacraments, in a tongue not understood by the people.

Article XVI—Of the Sacraments

Sacraments ordained of Christ are not only badges or tokens of Christian men's profession, but rather they are certain signs of grace, and God's good will toward us, by which he doth work invisibly in us, and doth not only quicken, but also strengthen and confirm, our faith in him.

There are two Sacraments ordained of Christ our Lord in the Gospel; that is to say, Baptism and the Supper of the Lord.

Those five commonly called sacraments, that is to say, confirmation, penance, orders, matrimony, and extreme unction, are not to be counted for Sacraments of the Gospel; being such as have partly grown out of the corrupt following of the apostles, and partly are states of life allowed in the Scriptures, but yet have not the like nature of Baptism and the Lord's Supper, because they have not any visible sign or ceremony ordained of God.

The Sacraments were not ordained of Christ to be gazed upon, or to be carried about; but that we should duly use them. And in such only as worthily receive the same, they have a wholesome effect or operation; but they that receive them unworthily, purchase to themselves condemnation, as St. Paul saith.

Article XVII — Of Baptism

Baptism is not only a sign of profession and mark of difference whereby Christians are distinguished from others that are not baptized; but it is also a sign of regeneration or the new birth. The Baptism of young children is to be retained in the Church.

Article XVIII — Of the Lord's Supper

The Supper of the Lord is not only a sign of the love that Christians ought to have among themselves one to another, but rather is a sacrament of our redemption by Christ's death; insomuch that, to such as rightly, worthily, and with faith receive the same, the bread which we break is a partaking of the body of Christ; and likewise the cup of blessing is a partaking of the blood of Christ.

Transubstantiation, or the change of the substance of bread and wine in the Supper of our Lord, cannot be proved by Holy Writ, but is repugnant to the plain words of Scripture, overthroweth the nature of a sacrament, and hath given occasion to many superstitions.

The body of Christ is given, taken, and eaten in the Supper, only after a heavenly and spiritual manner. And the mean whereby the body of Christ is received and eaten in the Supper is faith.

The Sacrament of the Lord's Supper was not by Christ's ordinance reserved, carried about, lifted up, or worshiped.

Article XIX — Of Both Kinds

The cup of the Lord is not to be denied to the lay people; for both the parts of the Lord's Supper, by Christ's ordinance and commandment, ought to be administered to all Christians alike.

Article XX — Of the One Oblation of Christ, Finished upon the Cross

The offering of Christ, once made, is that perfect redemption, propitiation, and satisfaction for all the sins of the whole world, both original and actual; and there is none other satisfaction for sin but that alone. Wherefore the sacrifice of masses, in the which it is commonly said that the priest doth offer Christ for the quick and the dead, to have remission of pain or guilt, is a blasphemous fable and dangerous deceit.

Article XXI — Of the Marriage of Ministers

The ministers of Christ are not commanded by God's law either to vow the estate of single life, or to abstain from marriage; therefore it is lawful for them, as for all other Christians, to marry at their own discretion, as they shall judge the same to serve best to godliness.

Article XXII — Of the Rites and Ceremonies of Churches

It is not necessary that rites and ceremonies should in all places be the same, or exactly alike; for they have been always different, and may be changed according to the diversity of countries, times, and men's manners, so that nothing be ordained against God's Word. Whosoever, through his private judgment, willingly and purposely doth openly break the rites and ceremonies of the church to which he belongs, which are not repugnant to the Word of God, and are ordained and approved by common authority, ought to be rebuked openly, that others may fear to do the like, as one that offendeth against the common order of the church, and woundeth the consciences of weak brethren.

Every particular church may ordain, change, or abolish rites and ceremonies, so that all things may be done to edification.

THE EVANGELICAL UNITED BRETHREN CONFESSION OF FAITH

Article V — The Church

We believe the Christian Church is the community of all true believers under the Lordship of Christ. We believe it is one, holy, apostolic and catholic. It is the redemptive fellowship in which the Word of God is preached by men divinely called, and the sacraments are duly administered according to Christ's own appointment. Under the discipline of the Holy Spirit the Church exists for the maintenance of worship, the edification of believers and the redemption of the world.

Article VI — The Sacraments

We believe the Sacraments, ordained by Christ, are symbols and pledges of the Christian's profession and of God's love toward us. They are means of grace by which God works invisibly in us, quickening, strengthening and confirming our faith in him. Two Sacraments are ordained by Christ our Lord, namely Baptism and the Lord's Supper.

We believe Baptism signifies entrance into the household of faith, and is a symbol of repentance and inner cleansing from sin, a representation of the new birth in Christ Jesus and a mark of Christian discipleship.

We believe children are under the atonement of Christ and as heirs of the Kingdom of God are acceptable subjects for Christian Baptism. Children of believing parents through Baptism become the special responsibility of the Church. They should be nurtured and led to personal acceptance of Christ, and by profession of faith confirm their Baptism.

We believe the Lord's Supper is a representation of our redemption, a memorial of the sufferings and death of Christ, and a token of love and union which Christians have with Christ and with one another. Those who rightly, worthily and in faith eat the broken bread and drink the blessed cup partake of the body and blood of Christ in a spiritual manner until he comes.

Article XIII — Public Worship

We believe divine worship is the duty and privilege of man who, in the presence of God, bows in adoration, humility and dedication. We believe divine worship is essential to the life of the Church, and that the assembling of the people of God for such worship is necessary to Christian fellowship and spiritual growth.

We believe the order of public worship need not be the same in all places but may be modified by the church according to circumstances and the needs of men. It should be in a language and form understood by the people, consistent with the Holy Scriptures to the edification of all, and in accordance with the order and Discipline of the Church.

Article XIV — The Lord's Day

We believe the Lord's Day is divinely ordained for private and public worship, for rest from unnecessary work, and should be devoted to spiritual improvement, Christian fellowship and service. It is commemorative of our Lord's resurrection and is an emblem of our eternal rest. It is essential to the permanence and growth of the Christian Church, and important to the welfare of the civil community.

THE ARTICLES OF FAITH

13. The Church

We believe the Christian Church is the community of all true believers under the Lordship of Christ. It is a unified, holy, apostolic, and universal (catholic) redemptive fellowship in which the Word of God is preached and the Sacraments administered. Under the direction of the Holy Spirit the Church exists for the worship of God, the nurturing of believers, and the redemption of the world.

14. Purgatory

We believe the doctrine of purgatory, the priestly pronouncing of pardon, the adoration of images and relics, and the veneration and invocation of the saints in prayer have no foundation in scripture and are not followed by us.

15. The Language of Worship

We believe, following the custom of the primitive church, that the language of worship, public prayer, and the sacraments is to be that which the people understand.

16. The Sacraments

We believe that the Sacraments are symbols of our Christian profession and signs of God's love toward us. They are "means of Grace" by which God works invisibly in us strengthening and confirming our faith in him. The two Sacraments ordained by Christ our Lord are Baptism and the Lord's Supper.

17. Baptism

We believe that Baptism signifies entrance into the Christian community, and is a symbol of repentance and inner cleansing from sin, a representation of the new birth in Jesus Christ, and a mark of Christian discipleship. Since children are accepted by Christ as heirs of the Kingdom of God, they may also be baptized, but their parents are to be believers and members of the Church themselves. The Church has a special responsibility to nurture and lead its children to confirm their faith and make a personal profession of faith in Christ.

18. The Lord's Supper

We believe the Lord's Supper is a symbol of our redemption through Christ's suffering and death on the cross. It is a sign of the unity and love that Christians have with Christ and one another. The transformation of the elements of bread and wine into the body and blood of Christ cannot be proved in Scripture. Those who eat the broken bread and drink from grape juice in faith and love partake of the body and blood of Christ in a spiritual manner until he comes. The elements are not to be carried about, lifted up, or worshiped.

19. The Elements of Bread and Grape Juice

We believe that both elements of the Lord's Supper, by Christ's own command, are to be administered to clergy and all Christians alike. (Grape juice is used rather than wine because of our long-standing emphasis on abstinence from alcoholic beverages and our consideration for the special problems of the alcoholic.)

20. Reconciliation through Christ

We believe the offering Christ made on the cross is a perfect and sufficient sacrifice for the sins of the whole world, redeeming us from all sin, both original and particular, so that no other satisfaction for sin is required or necessary.

21. The Marriage of Pastors

We believe that Pastors are not commanded by God to live the single life, or to abstain from marriage; therefore, it is as lawful for them to marry as for all other Christians. They must decide for themselves whether they can best serve God through the single life or marriage.

22. Public Worship

We believe that public worship is the duty and privilege of all persons, who are to bow in adoration, humility, and dedication in the presence of God. Worship is essential to the life of the Church, and the assembling of the people of God for such worship is necessary for Christian fellowship and spiritual growth. The order of public worship need not be the same in all places, but may be modified by the Church to meet local circumstances and the needs of the people. Every particular church is free to use, change, or abolish various rites and ceremonies as long as everything remains consistent with scripture and is done to nurture the people of God.

26. The Lord's Day

We believe the Lord's Day is ordained of God for private and public worship and for rest from unnecessary work. It should be devoted to spiritual improvement, Christian fellowship, and service to others. It is a memorial of our Lord's Resurrection and a symbol of our eternal rest. It is essential to the permanence and growth of the Christian Church, and important to the welfare of the civil community.

THE CHRISTIAN YEAR

The United Methodist Church follows the Ecumenical Christian Year. This year is divided into Seasons of various lengths rather than in months. We observe this Christian calendar to remind ourselves that God is the Lord and giver of life and that every year we have on earth is a gift from Him. The Christian Year enables us to recreate and relive the "cycle" of our Redemption in Christ.

The Christian Year is divided into two halves. The first half follows the events in the life of Christ and runs from ADVENT through EASTER. It teaches us what God has done for us through His Son Jesus Christ. This is our JUSTIFICATION. The second half relates the teachings of the Church to us as believers in Jesus Christ and is called PENTECOST. During this portion of the Christian Year we learn what we shall do to fulfill our responsibilities as the people of God. This is our SANCTIFICATION.

OUR JUSTIFICATION

Advent

The Christian Year begins with the Season of Advent, the four weeks preceding Christmas. Advent means "coming." This is the Season when we look forward to our Lord's coming. Many years before Jesus was born in Bethlehem, the Old Testament prophets told God's people that the Lord would come to dwell among them. During Advent we share this age-old expectation of God's people as they waited for His coming. We remember that He comes to dwell in us as well as among us. Advent points especially to the glory of Christ's second coming. The increasing number of candles, one each week, tell the story of this expectation. The flames tell us of the light that God has sent into the darkness of our sin. Purple was the traditional color for Advent, symbolizing the spirit of repentance called for by the prophets as humanity waited for the coming of its Redeemer; but today, the optional color of blue has been given to distinguish this as a Season of Joy.

Christmas

"For God so loved the world that He gave His only-begotten Son." This is the gift of Christmas. All of God's love, all of His judgment, and all of His power are given in the form of a baby lying on a bed of straw. This was the way in which God chose to give us our King. The manger tells of the fulfillment of our expectation. The waiting of Advent is over: God is with us. A Christ Candle on Christmas Eve symbolizes for us that Christ is the Light of the world. Every day is Christmas when the Light of Christ shines into the darkness of our sin. We are reminded that "it is no longer I who live, but Christ who lives in me." White is the color for Christmas.

Epiphany

The Epiphany Season begins twelve days after Christmas, but not necessarily on a Sunday. The word epiphany means "manifestation of God." On Christmas God appeared in the world as a human being, in the baby Jesus. The symbol of the star comes to us from the story of the wise men who came to see the baby Jesus. God led them by means of the Star from a far country to Bethlehem where Jesus was born. That is why the story of the wise men is read as this Season begins. The other Gospel passages that are read during this Season tell of the miracles Jesus performed which showed that He was truly God. The wise men were Gentiles. Christ came so that all people might know of God's wondrous love. We, as members of His Church, have been given the task of proclaiming this message of Joy to all the world, even to the most remote corners of the earth. The color for this Season is Green.

Lent

This Season includes the six weeks before Easter Sunday, beginning with the day we call Ash Wednesday. The Lenten Season serves to remind us of the time in Jesus' life when He took upon Himself the sin of His people. Lent is also a time when we prepare for our resurrection with Christ on Easter morning. Most important in this preparation for newness of life in Christ is the recognition of our old life of sin. For this reason Lent is a special time for self examination and repentance. By our self examination we are led to repent of our sins and depend solely upon the mercy of God in Jesus Christ who has given us the assurance that, "though your sins be as scarlet, they shall be white as snow." The cup on our symbol brings to mind Christ's prayer in Gethsemane; "...remove this cup from me." Jesus was speaking of His suffering as the cup which He did not want to drink. However, He was crucified because God had chosen that He should die instead of us. And when Jesus was crucified, His blood was shed. The blood flowing from the cup down over the globe reminds us again that, "God so loved the world that He gave His only-begotten Son." The color for this Season of Repentance is Purple.

Easter

Easter is the answer of God to the sin of His people. Because God raised His Son from the dead, sinless and eternal, so shall those who believe in Him be sinless and eternal. Because Christ lives we also shall live. In God's sight our sin is dead in the grave and we have life eternal. The bright sun is a symbol of life because without the sun there would be no life on this earth. The sun also reminds us of Easter morning and the Risen

119

Christ. The empty cross that appears in the center of the sun symbolizes that our hope lies in Jesus who rose from the dead. Death has been swallowed up in victory on this great day, and Christ has risen like the morning sun. The light which He gives cannot be overcome, and the life which comes from Him shall not perish. This is the Christian hope of Easter.

OUR SANCTIFICATION

Pentecost

The Season of Pentecost begins on the seventh Sunday after Easter, and it is the time which symbolizes the coming of the holy Spirit. Before Jesus returned to live with God the Father, He told His disciples that He would send His Holy Spirit. The Spirit would show His people the tasks they were to do and would give them the power to accomplish them. We are told of the coming of the Holy Spirit to the disciples in the second chapter of the Book of Acts. This event, Pentecost, is known as the Birthday of the Christian Church. Even to this day the same Spirit enables the Christian Church to serve its Lord by calling us to faith in the Triune God and to fellowship with other believers. The seven flames on our symbol represent the seven gifts of the Spirit which God gives to His people. These gifts are wisdom, understanding, knowledge, counsel, fortitude, piety and fear of the Lord. By these gifts of the Spirit we are enabled to grow in faith. The color for the Season of Pentecost is Red on the Day of Pentecost, but then it turns Green for the rest of the Season. This long Season was once divided up by the United Methodist Church into Pentecost and Kingdomtide; but to follow the Ecumenical Community, we have given up Kingdomtide. Some Churches may still observe it, and others may change the color to Red in September to symbolize the emphasis on the Kingdom of God, as was the purpose of the Season of Kingdomtide.

Trinity Sunday

Trinity Sunday is not the beginning of a new Season; rather, it occurs on the first Sunday after Pentecost. It celebrates the union of Father, Son, and Holy Spirit as God. This follows the portion of the Christian Year when we have emphasized the three persons of God in a more individual way. Advent tells us of the promise of God the Father and Creator; Christmas through Easter focuses on the redemption through the Son; Pentecost celebrates the gift of the Holy Spirit to the Church. Now we celebrate the oneness of the three persons. The Triangle is symbolic of the Holy Trinity: God the Father; God the Son; and God the Holy Spirit. The green plant form is representative of growth and, hence, gives this special day of the year its symbolic color, green. As Christians our growth is solely dependent upon the Triune God in whom we "live and move and have our being." From this day until Advent begins, the Church looks at the sanctification of its people; the emphasis is on our growth and maturity as Christians. During this period the Gospel texts that are read to us in Church are lessons about the growth of the Kingdom of God and the growth of ourselves as Christians. It is interesting to note that this time of the Christian Year parallels the Season of maturity in nature. So too, must we as Christians, grow and mature in the faith into which we have been received. This is our Sanctification as God's people, for we look forward to the day when,"The Kingdom of the world has become the Kingdom of our Lord and of His Christ, and He shall reign for ever and ever." (Revelation 11:15).

9. THE SOCIAL PRINCIPLES

Personal and Social Holiness

The Goal

The Controversial Social Principles

Marriage

Divorce

Abortion

Human Sexuality

Equal Rights Regardless of Sexual Orientation

Alcohol and Other Drugs

Military Service

The Death Penalty

War and the Christian

PERSONAL AND SOCIAL HOLINESS

The Historical Development

1. Early Methodism opposed the slave trade, smuggling, and inhumane treatment of prisoners. Refer to the General Rules.

2. It was after the General Conference of 1840 turned its face against the abolitionists, not even allowing a minority report, that the Wesleyan Methodist Church withdrew to establish a new denomination.

3. The great break in American Methodism came in 1843/44, when the slavery issue led to the formation of the Methodist Episcopal Church, South. Another issue had to do with holiness, a doctrine emphasized by Wesley.

4. In 1860 the Free Methodist Church split off from the Methodist Episcopal Church, North. The issue was over three freedoms: (1) freedom from slavery, (2) freedom from rented pews, and (3) freedom from secret societies, such as the Masons. The Free Methodists wanted to adhere more to the early principles of Methodism.

5. The first Social Creed was established in 1908 by the Methodist Episcopal Church, North, followed by the Methodist Episcopal Church, South, and the Methodist Protestant Church. The three churches finally merged in 1939.

6. The social Principles were established in 1946 by the new Evangelical United Brethren, a merger of the United Brethren and the Evangelical Association (Church).

7. The Social Principles were revised in 1972, following the merger of the Evangelical United Brethren and The Methodist Church in 1968.

8. The purpose was to speak to human issues in the contemporary world from a sound Biblical and theological foundation (in the prophetic tradition).

9. The Preamble symbolizes three things: (1) an affirmation in the triune God, (2) the need to confess sins with the need for salvation, and (3) a commitment to personal and social holiness.

The Social Creed

We believe in God, Creator of the world; and in Jesus Christ, the Redeemer of creation. We believe in the Holy Spirit, through whom we acknowledge God's gifts, and we repent of our sin in misusing these gifts to idolatrous ends.

We affirm the natural world as God's handiwork and dedicate ourselves to its preservation, enhancement, and faithful use by humankind.

We joyfully receive for ourselves and others the blessings of community, sexuality, marriage, and the family.

We commit ourselves to the rights of men, women, children, youth, young adults, the aging, and people with disabilities; to improvement of the quality of life; and to the rights and dignity of all persons.

We believe in the right and duty of persons to work for the glory of God and the good of themselves and others and in the protection of their welfare in so doing; in the rights to property as a trust from God, collective bargaining, and responsible consumption; and in the elimination of economic and social distress.

We dedicate ourselves to peace throughout the world, to the rule of justice and law among nations, and to individual freedom for all people of the world.

We believe in the present and final triumph of God's Word in human affairs and gladly accept our commission to manifest the life of the gospel in the world. Amen.

The World Methodist Social Affirmation

We believe in God, creator of the world and of all people; and in Jesus Christ, incarnate among us, who died and rose again; and in the Holy Spirit, present with us to guide, strengthen, and comfort.

We rejoice in every sign of God's kingdom: in the upholding of human dignity and community; in every expression of love, justice, and reconciliation; in each act of self-giving on behalf of others; in the abundance of God's gifts entrusted to us that all may have enough; in all responsible use of the earth's resources.

Glory be to God on high; and on earth, peace.

THE CONTROVERSIAL SOCIAL PRINCIPLES

Marriage

We affirm the sanctity of the marriage covenant that is expressed in love, mutual support, personal commitment, and shared fidelity between a man and a woman. We believe that God's blessing rests upon such marriage, whether or not there are children of the union. We reject social norms that assume different standards for women than for men in marriage. We support laws in civil society that define marriage as the union of one man and one woman.

Divorce

God's plan is for lifelong, faithful marriage. The church must be on the forefront of premarital and postmarital counseling in order to create and preserve strong marriages. However, when a married couple is estranged beyond reconciliation, even after thoughtful consideration and counsel, divorce is a regrettable alternative in the midst of brokenness. We grieve over the devastating emotional, spiritual, and economic consequences of divorce for all involved and are concerned about high divorce rates.

It is recommended that methods of mediation be used to minimize the adversarial nature and fault-finding that are often part of our current judicial processes. Although divorce publicly declares that a marriage no longer exists, other covenantal relationships resulting from the marriage remain, such as the nurture and support of children and extended family ties. We urge respectful negotiations in deciding the custody of minor children and support the consideration of either or both parents for this responsibility in that custody not be reduced to financial support, control, or manipulation and retaliation. The welfare of each child is the most important consideration. Divorce does not preclude a new marriage. We encourage an intentional commitment of the Church and society to minister compassionately to those in the process of divorce, as well as members of divorced and remarried families, in a community of faith where God's grace is shared by all.

Abortion

The beginning of life and the ending of life are the God-given boundaries of human existence. While individuals have always had some degree of control over when they would die, they now have the awesome power to determine when and even whether new individuals will be born.

Our belief in the sanctity of unborn human life makes us reluctant to approve abortion. But we are equally bound to respect the sacredness of the life and well-being of the mother, for whom devastating damage may result from an unacceptable pregnancy. In continuity with past Christian teaching, we recognize tragic conflicts of life with life that may justify abortion, and in such cases we support the legal option of abortion under proper medical procedures. We cannot affirm abortion as an acceptable means of birth control, and we unconditionally reject it as a means of gender selection.

We oppose the use of late-term abortion known as dilation and extraction (partial-birth abortion) and call for the end of this practice except when the physical life of the mother is in danger and no other medical procedure is available, or in the case of severe fetal anomalies incompatible with life. We call all Christians to a searching and prayerful inquiry into the sorts of conditions that may warrant abortion. We commit our Church to continue to provide nurturing ministries to those who terminate a pregnancy, to those in the midst of a crisis pregnancy, and to those who give birth. We particularly encourage the Church, the government, and social service agencies to support and facilitate the option of adoption. (See ¶ 161.K.)

Governmental laws and regulations do not provide all the guidance required by the informed Christian conscience. Therefore, a decision concerning abortion should be made only after thoughtful and prayerful consideration by the parties involved, with medical, pastoral, and other appropriate counsel.

Human Sexuality

We recognize that sexuality is God's good gift to all persons. We believe persons may be fully human only when that gift is acknowledged and affirmed by themselves, the church, and society. We call all persons to the disciplined, responsible fulfillment of themselves, others, and society in the stewardship of this gift. We also recognize our limited understanding of this complex gift and encourage the medical, theological, and social science disciplines to combine in a determined effort to understand human sexuality more completely. We call the Church to take the leadership role in bringing together these disciplines to address this most complex issue. Further, within the context of our understanding of this gift of God, we recognize that God challenges us to find responsible, committed, and loving forms of expression.

Although all persons are sexual beings whether or not they are married, sexual relations are only clearly affirmed in the marriage bond. Sex may become exploitative within as well as outside marriage. We reject all sexual expressions that damage or destroy the humanity God has given us as birthright, and we affirm only that sexual expression that enhances that same humanity. We believe that sexual relations where one or both partners are exploitative, abusive, or promiscuous are beyond the parameters of acceptable Christian behavior and are ultimately destructive to individuals, families, and the social order.

We deplore all forms of the commercialization and exploitation of sex, with their consequent cheapening and degradation of human personality. We call for strict global enforcement of laws prohibiting the sexual exploitation or use of children by adults and encourage efforts to hold perpetrators legally and financially responsible. We call for the establishment of adequate protective services, guidance, and counseling opportunities for children thus abused. We insist that all persons, regardless of age, gender, marital status, or sexual orientation, are entitled to have their human and civil rights ensured.

We recognize the continuing need for full, positive, age-appropriate and factual sex education opportunities for children, young people, and adults. The Church offers a unique opportunity to give quality guidance and education in this area.

Homosexual persons no less than heterosexual persons are individuals of sacred worth. All persons need the ministry and guidance of the church in their struggles for human fulfillment, as well as the spiritual and emotional care of a fellowship that enables reconciling relationships with God, with others, and with self. The United Methodist Church does not condone the practice of homosexuality and considers this practice incompatible with Christian teaching. We affirm that God's grace is available to all, and we will seek to live together in Christian community. We implore families and churches not to reject or condemn lesbian and gay members and friends. We commit ourselves to be in ministry for and with all persons.[1]

Equal Rights Regardless of Sexual Orientation

Certain basic human rights and civil liberties are due all persons. We are committed to supporting those rights and liberties for homosexual persons.

We see a clear issue of simple justice in protecting their rightful claims where they have shared material resources, pensions, guardian relationships, mutual powers of attorney, and other such lawful claims typically attendant to contractual relationships that involve shared129 contributions, responsibilities, and liabilities, and equal protection before the law.

[1] See Judicial Council Decision 702.

Moreover, we support efforts to stop violence and other forms of coercion against gays and lesbians. We also commit ourselves to social witness against the coercion and marginalization of former homosexuals.

Alcohol and Other Drugs

We affirm our long-standing support of abstinence from alcohol as a faithful witness to God's liberating and redeeming love for persons. We support abstinence from the use of any illegal drugs. Since the use of illegal drugs, as well as illegal and problematic use of alcohol, is a major factor in crime, disease, death, and family dysfunction, we support educational programs as well as other prevention strategies encouraging abstinence from illegal drug use and, with regard to those who choose to consume alcoholic beverages, judicious use with deliberate and intentional restraint, with Scripture as a guide.

Millions of living human beings are testimony to the beneficial consequences of therapeutic drug use, and millions of others are testimony to the detrimental consequences of drug misuse. We encourage wise policies relating to the availability of potentially beneficial or potentially damaging prescription and over-the-counter drugs; we urge that complete information about their use and misuse be readily available to both doctor and patient. We support the strict administration of laws regulating the sale and distribution of alcohol and controlled substances. We support regulations that protect society from users of drugs of any kind, including alcohol, where it can be shown that a clear and present social danger exists. Drug-dependent persons and their family members, including those who are assessed or diagnosed as dependent on alcohol, are individuals of infinite human worth deserving of treatment, rehabilitation, and ongoing life-changing recovery. Misuse or abuse may also require intervention, in order to prevent progression into dependence. Because of the frequent interrelationship between alcohol abuse and mental illness, we call upon legislators and health care providers to make available appropriate mental illness treatment and rehabilitation for drug-dependent persons. We commit ourselves to assisting those who suffer from abuse or dependence, and their families, in finding freedom through Jesus Christ and in finding good opportunities for treatment, for ongoing counseling, and for reintegration into society.

Military Service

We deplore war and urge the peaceful settlement of all disputes among nations. From the beginning, the Christian conscience has struggled with the harsh realities of violence and war, for these evils clearly frustrate God's loving purposes for humankind. We yearn for the day when there will be no more war and people will live together in peace and justice.

Some of us believe that war, and other acts of violence, are never acceptable to Christians. We also acknowledge that many Christians believe that, when peaceful alternatives have failed, the force of arms may regretfully be preferable to unchecked aggression, tyranny and genocide. We honor the witness of pacifists who will not allow us to become complacent about war and violence. We also respect those who support the use of force, but only in extreme situations and only when the need is clear beyond reasonable doubt, and through appropriate international organizations. We urge the establishment of the rule of law in international affairs as a means of elimination of war, violence, and coercion in these affairs.

We reject national policies of enforced military service as incompatible with the gospel. We acknowledge the agonizing tension created by the demand for military service by national governments. We urge all young adults to seek the counsel of the Church as they reach a conscientious decision concerning the nature of their responsibility as citizens. Pastors are called upon to be available for counseling with all young adults who face conscription, including those who conscientiously refuse to cooperate with a system of conscription.

We support and extend the ministry of the Church to those persons who conscientiously oppose all war, or any particular war, and who therefore refuse to serve in the armed forces or to cooperate with systems of military conscription. We also support and extend the Church's ministry to those persons who conscientiously choose to serve in the armed forces or to accept alternative service. As Christians we are aware that neither the way of military action, nor the way of inaction is always righteous before God.

The Death Penalty

We believe the death penalty denies the power of Christ to redeem, restore and transform all human beings. The United Methodist Church is deeply concerned about crime throughout the world and the value of any life taken by a murder or homicide. We believe all human life is sacred and created by God and therefore, we must see all human life as significant and valuable. When governments implement the death penalty (capital punishment), then the life of the convicted person is devalued and all possibility of change in that person's life ends. We believe in the resurrection of Jesus Christ and that the possibility of reconciliation with Christ comes through repentance. This gift of reconciliation is offered to all individuals without exception and gives all life new dignity and sacredness. For this reason, we oppose the death penalty (capital punishment) and urge its elimination from all criminal codes.

WAR AND THE CHRISTIAN

ATTITUDES TOWARDS WAR

Roland Bainton has suggested three types of attitudes toward war. These attitudes all reflect different attitudes towards violence. These attitudes concerning violence all have to do with whether "the end justifies the means used."

The Crusade. The first of these attitudes is that of the crusade. This position clearly states that the end does indeed justify the means—any means. One sees his own cause as being justified by God or some secular ideology. This cause justifies whatever means might be used, for the enemy is seen as being totally evil. Therefore the enemy must be destroyed.

The Just War. Augustine was the first theologian to develop the Just War criteria. He said that men sought peace by waging war. The end was peace, and so we find in this position that only some means are justified by an end. A Just War is one in which the ruler defends the nation from aggression or compels the enemy to make reparation for wrongs committed against his nation. A Just War can never be fought for conquest, glory, or wealth; but rather, a Just War must be fought for the sake of peace and the restoration of relationships.

Pacifism. This was the position of the early Church until the time of Augustine, and it taught that no end justifies any means. War is against the will of God, and thus Christians are not to resort to it. Today Pacifism can be accepted for several reasons such as (1) religious, (2) philosophical, or (3) even practical. It can take the form of active resistance, or it can be a complete withdrawal from the conflict. All pacifists are united in refusing to use violence against the enemy. Christians usually draw on the Sermon on the Mount (Matthew 5-7) and Jesus' command to love the enemy (Matthew 5:43-48) to support Pacifism.

THE JUST WAR

Judaism has never rejected war. Islam has accepted the possibility of the Crusade. Christianity has been more uncertain, and has usually supported either Pacifism or the Just War. Since the Just War finds more support than the other positions, it is this concept that needs the most explanation.

Definition Of The Just War. Jacques Ellul in his book, *Violence*, suggests that there are seven conditions that must be present if a war to be considered as Just. They are as follows: (1) The cause fought for must be itself Just. (2) The purpose of the warring power must remain just while

132

hostilities go on. (3) War must be truly the last resort, all peaceful means having been exhausted. (4) The methods employed during the war to vanquish the foe must themselves be Just. (5) The benefits they can reasonably be expected to bring for humanity must be greater than the evils provoked by the war itself. (6) Victory must be assured. (7) The peace concluded at the end of the war must be Just and of such nature as to prevent a new war.

The Just War Criteria. Let us now examine the more important criteria mentioned above and try to systematize them.

The Just Cause

The cause has to do with preventing a wrong or making something right. The cause is usually related to self-defense, but could also be related to aggression if the intention is to make right a wrong. Usually the Just Cause must be related either to self-defense or human rights. Since human rights can easily become an issue leading to "The Crusade" most nations see self-defense as the most important reason for going to war.

The Just Intention

Once it has decided that war must be fought, there is still the question of one's real intention. Why is this war being waged? One should not aim at destroying the enemy, nor should one fight for the purpose of aggression and retaliation. The aim of the war should be to restore peace. A Just Intention aims at restoring relations between the two communities, and does not aim at destroying the other community. If a nation feels that it must fight a war of aggression it does not hold on to the other nation's land after the war is over. The aim is making right a wrong, and this cannot involve another wrong. The nation fighting a Just War does not intend to destroy the other nation, nor does it take land away from it.

The Competent Authority

This third criterion involves the right to call a nation into war. Who has that right? It is not enough to say that the legal ruler or authorities have that right. One must also take into consideration whether or not such rulers or authorities enjoy social support. Do the people in the nation really support their rulers? The rulers must enjoy both legal and social authority, or they cannot be considered as competent authorities.

Just Conduct of the War

The conduct of the war must also be Just. Naturally this criterion already assumes that there is a reasonable hope of success in winning the War, and that the war is being fought as a last resort. No other alternative remains, but yet there are certain principles which must be followed in the conduct of that war.

The Principle of Proportion. The first principle of conduct is that of proportion. Will the good outweigh the bad effects of the war? If greater harm is done by waging the war than by enduring the evil which caused the war, then the war cannot be justified. It is also important to calculate the advantages and disadvantages of each battle. It may be better to leave a city in tact, than to destroy it by winning the battle. One must ask how important this particular battle really is to the total war effort.

The Principle of Discrimination. The second important principle of conduct has to do with discriminating between soldiers and civilians or between non-military and military targets., Only soldiers are to be killed, and only military targets are to be bombed. It is realized that one cannot always make such fine distinctions in the heat of war, but this is to be the intention of the Just War. Civilians will be destroyed and hospitals and schools will be destroyed, but this must never be the aim of those who mistakenly destroy them. If one destroys civilians and non-military targets intentionally, then such conduct does not fall into the category of the Just War.

Problems with Just War Criteria. Two recent events have made the Just War Theory difficult to maintain, and they are the invention of nuclear weapons and the emergence of insurgency warfare.

Nuclear Weapons

Nuclear weapons not only destroy more than military targets, that is their very intent. They were not created to distinguish between soldiers and civilians, but to destroy everything in sight. When used on cities, they cannot make distinctions between what is used for military purposes and what is clearly non-military, they destroy the whole city.

Insurgency Warfare

Insurgency warfare considers everyone to be part of the war effort, and this means that there is no difference between soldiers and civilians. Everyone is considered to be a soldier, even though many do not wear uniforms. This problem will be taken up again as we deal with the problem of revolution.

JUST WAR AND INSURGENCY WARFARE

I find two or three just war criteria particularly helpful in lifting up some of the problems that insurgency or revolutionary movements do not deal with adequately. The first one is the question of a **competent authority**. Let us look briefly at this first one before turning to the others.

There is no doubt that justified reasons are given for a revolt against an oppressive government, but at the same time. there is a need to establish competent authority in order to exercise power and lead a revolution. Such authority ought to have some kind of basis in the community for which that authority is being exercised. Juan Segundo suggests that revolutionaries may have to begin their work without much popular support and that they might even have to take brutal measures against the people in order to make the situation so bad that the people will be motivated to join the campaign against what the revolutionaries themselves have made into an unbearable situation. The question I would raise at this point is: Can Christians support this kind of an approach to establishing authority? Even if such methods were accepted to get the revolution moving, how can we know that the leaders of such a revolution are the right ones to be leading it? That they claim to be able to perceive God's activity in the world is not enough. That might be sufficient reason for one to speak out prophetically, but it is not enough to give one authority to lead a revolution or become the head of a government. Establishing the criteria for taking such leadership is necessary for anyone advocating violent revolutionary activity.

A second just war criterion that points to a problem in violent revolutionary activity is the **principle of discrimination** that is usually included under the broader category of **just conduct**. It has to do with whether the war can be conducted in a just manner. The principle of discrimination forbids any intent to harm noncombatants and destroy their society. Revolutionary activity, however, takes place among and between the people and denies the validity that anyone can be a noncombatant. Roger Shinn points out that "guerrilla warfare" denies the principle of discrimination just as truly as does "nuclear war," though certainly not on so grand a scale. The rejection of this principle on the part of revolutionaries is well known. Revolutionaries—at least in the beginning —avoid direct confrontation with military forces and attack instead the civil structures of society. They attempt to undermine public confidence in the government and demonstrate to the people that the government is unable to provide protection for them. They direct their attack against those persons whose services might otherwise improve society, thus increasing the need for violent revolutionary change. The problem, however, is not only that revolutionaries violate the principle of discrimination or noncombatant immunity, but that the reason they do it is because they interpret the conflict in ultimate terms. The situation is serious and they are not playing around. This is the reason that moral limits tend to fall away as they struggle to destroy the enemy, whom they perceive as totally evil. When they perceive and conduct the struggle in ultimate terms, they tend to evoke a corresponding response from the enemy and the conflict takes on a religious character. This is the danger I perceive in the approach taken by political and liberation theologians, They reject the just war criterion of noncombatant immunity. No one can be immune from the conflict. Everyone has to be involved. Not to support one side means that you support the other.

One final criterion might be mentioned and that is the one concerning **last resort**. Those advocating violent revolutionary activity rarely use the principle of last resort. The cause seems just and the timing right. Jacques Ellul, however, warns:

> The Christian can never entertain this idea of "last resort." He understands that for the others it may be so, because they place all their hopes in this world and the meaning of this world. But for the Christian, violence can be at most a second-last resort.

10. THE CHURCH AND THE WORLD

Historical Relationships
The Methodist Articles of Religion
The Evangelical United Brethren Confession of Faith
The Articles of Faith
The United Methodist Church
The Three Branches
The Five Jurisdictions
The Local Church
The Local Church A
The Local Church B
Our Mission Statement
Make Disciples for Jesus Christ!

HISTORICAL RELATIONSHIPS

1. **The Church Dominates the State.** Sometimes the church has dominated the state. One of the great figures of the early church was Ambrose, Bishop of Milan. He was a close friend of Theodosius the Roman Emperor who was a Christian.

2. **Hostility between Church and State**. There have been times when the church was utterly independent of the state, and when the church claimed that it was acting under an authority to which the state was also subject. ... It is not rebellion or revolution. It comes from the highest kind of loyalty, but it comes from the conviction that the differences are gone when men stand in the presence of God, and that God's man must speak no matter who is listening. King, queen and commoner are all subjects of God.

3. **The Church is Subservient to the State**. There have been times when the church surrendered to the state and became subservient to the state. "A subservient church is a national disaster. It was said of Ambrose that he was 'the personified conscience of all that was best in the Roman Empire'. 'Who', he said to Theodosius, 'will dare to tell you the truth, if a priest does not dare?' The nation which has no independent church has lost its conscience."

4. **There is No Relationship between Church and State**. There have been times when the state refused the church any say at all in the affairs of the state, because the state held that such things were none of the church's business. "And the totalitarian states have no objection to religion so long as religion keeps its mouth shut about earth and confines itself to dreams of heaven—and that, of course, reduces the church to a status of sheer irrelevancy.

5. **There are Two Realms (Kingdoms).** Luther's view: He divides people into two groups and he divides life into two areas. There are believers who belong to the Kingdom of God and there are those who do not believe and belong to the kingdom of the world. If all men were true Christians, no king, lord, sword, or law would be necessary. They would do everything the law demands and more. It is impossible to rule the world by the gospel and its love. Christians need no law, but non-Christians do. Therefore the sword is necessary. As long as there are two kinds of people, those in and those not in the Kingdom of God, it is impossible to arrange society on the principles of Christian love. There must be law and

force; there must be the sword of the magistrate. You cannot govern an unchristian world by Christian love.[1]

THE METHODIST ARTICLES OF RELIGION

Article XXIII—Of the Rulers of the United States of America

The President, the Congress, the general assemblies, the governors, and the councils of state, as the delegates of the people, are the rulers of the United States of America, according to the division of power made to them by the Constitution of the United States and by the constitutions of their respective states. And the said states are a sovereign and independent nation, and ought not to be subject to any foreign jurisdiction.

Article XXIV—Of Christian Men's Goods

The riches and goods of Christians are not common as touching the right, title, and possession of the same, as some do falsely boast. Notwithstanding, every man ought, of such things as he possesseth, liberally to give alms to the poor, according to his ability.

Article XXV—Of a Christian Man's Oath

As we confess that vain and rash swearing is forbidden Christian men by our Lord Jesus Christ and James his apostle, so we judge that the Christian religion doth not prohibit, but that a man may swear when the magistrate requireth, in a cause of faith and charity, so it be done according to the prophet's teaching, in justice, judgment, and truth.

[The following provision was adopted by the Uniting Conference (1939). This statement seeks to interpret to our churches in foreign lands Article XXIII of the Articles of Religion. It is a legislative enactment but is not a part of the Constitution. (See Judicial Council Decisions 41, 176, and Decision 6, Interim Judicial Council.)]

Of the Duty of Christians to the Civil Authority

It is the duty of all Christians, and especially of all Christian ministers, to observe and obey the laws and commands of the governing or supreme authority of the country of which they are citizens or subjects or in which they reside, and to use all laudable means to encourage and enjoin obedience to the powers that be.

---

[1] William Barclay, *Ethics in a Permissive Society* (London: Collins Books, 1971), pp. 171ff.

THE EVANGELICAL UNITED BRETHREN CONFESSION OF FAITH

Article XV — The Christian and Property

We believe God is the owner of all things and that the individual holding of property is lawful and is a sacred trust under God. Private property is to be used for the manifestation of Christian love and liberality, and to support the Church's mission in the world. All forms of property, whether private, corporate or public, are to be held in solemn trust and used responsibly for human good under the sovereignty of God

Article XVI — Civil Government

We believe civil government derives its just powers from the sovereign God. As Christians we recognize the governments under whose protection we reside and believe such governments should be based on, and be responsible for, the recognition of human rights under God. We believe war and bloodshed are contrary to the gospel and spirit of Christ. We believe it is the duty of Christian citizens to give moral strength and purpose to their respective governments through sober, righteous and godly living.

THE ARTICLES OF FAITH

23. Civil Government

We believe civil government derives its just powers from God. As Christians we recognize the government of the United States under whose protection we reside and believe that this government should be based on, and responsible for, the human rights of its people under God. In turn as Christian citizens we have a responsibility to offer moral strength and purpose to our government through sober, righteous, and godly living.

24. Private Property

We believe God is the owner of all things. Individuals who "legally" own property do so as a sacred trust under God. Private property is to be used for the manifestation of Christian love and liberality, and to support the Church's mission in the world according to our ability. All forms of property, whether private, corporate or public, are to be held in solemn trust and used responsibly for human good under the sovereignty of God.

25. Oaths

Although we agree that it is forbidden in scripture to swear an oath falsely, we do believe that it is consistent with scripture to swear an oath in a court of law, where it must be done in faith and love to promote truth and justice.

THE UNITED METHODIST CHURCH

The United Methodist Church has a three-part structure, just as the Federal Government does. We also have a constituion and doctrinal standards that help determine who we are and how we live as United Methodists.

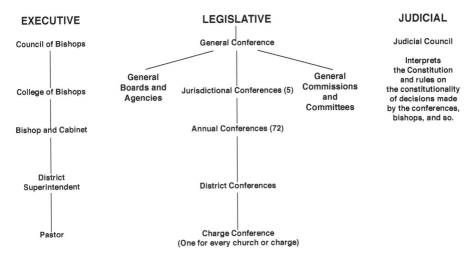

EXECUTIVE

Council of Bishops

College of Bishops

Bishop and Cabinet

District Superintendent

Pastor

LEGISLATIVE

General Conference

General Boards and Agencies

Jurisdictional Conferences (5)

General Commissions and Committees

Annual Conferences (72)

District Conferences

Charge Conference
(One for every church or charge)

JUDICIAL

Judicial Council

Interprets the Constitution and rules on the constitutionality of decisions made by the conferences, bishops, and so.

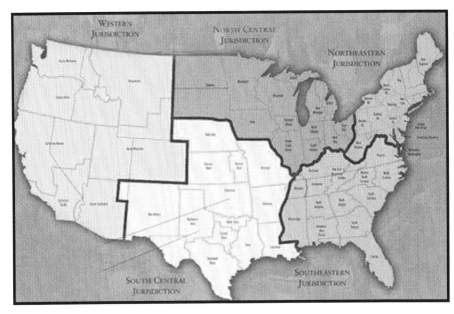

LOCAL CHURCH A

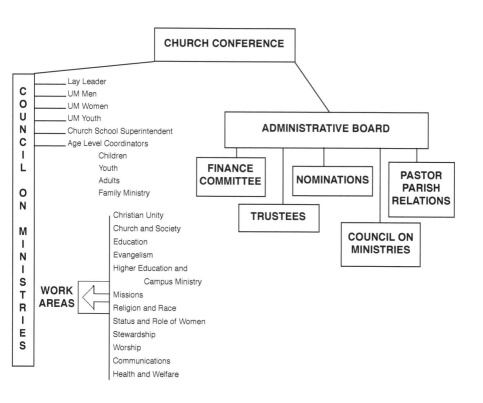

LOCAL CHURCH B

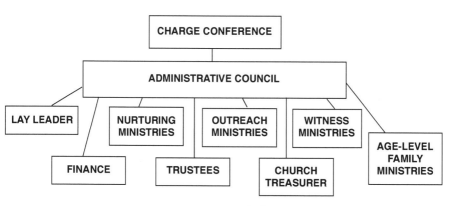

143

OUR MISSION STATEMENT

The mission of the Church is to make disciples of Jesus Christ
for the transformation of the world.

COVENANT PRAYER

I am no longer my own, but thine.
Put me to what thou wilt, rank me with whom thou wilt.
Put me to doing, put me to suffering.
Let me be employed by thee or laid aside for thee,
exalted for thee or brought low for thee.
Let me be full, let me be empty.
Let me have all things, let me have nothing.
I freely and heartily yield all things
to thy pleasure and disposal.
And now, O glorious and blessed God,
Father, Son, and Holy Spirit,
thou art mine, and I am thine. So be it.
And the covenant which I have made on earth,
let it be ratified in heaven. Amen.

OTHER BOOKS BY THE AUTHOR

BIBLE STUDY GUIDES

1. **The Bible as Sacred History:**
   Survey of the Whole Bible

2. **The Struggle with God:**
   Genesis through Deuteronomy

3. **Sacred Stories:**
   Joshua through Esther

4. **The Search for Wisdom:**
   Job through Ecclesiastes

5. **Time is Running Out:**
   Major and Minor Prophets

6. **Between the Testaments:**
   Books of the Apocrypha

7. **The Messengers:**
   The Four Gospels

8. **An Explosion of Faith:**
   Acts and Revelation

9. **The First E-Letters:**
   All of the Letters

10. **The Second Creation:**
    Revelation (Formatted: 6x9)

11. **A Vision of Hope:**
    Revelation: (Formatted 8.5x11)

12. **New Testament Photos 1**
    The Gospels

13. **New Testament Photos 2**
    The Letters

BOOKS

1. **Ignited for Mission:**
   A Call to Mission

2. **Reformulating the Mission of the Church:**
   A Theology of Missions

3. **Our Spiritual Senses:**
   The Five Spiritual Senses

4. **Our Spiritual Disciplines:**
   The Six Spiritual Disciplines

5. **The Ordinary Christian Experience:**
   Fourteen Ordinary Experiences

6. **Faith is a Choice:**
   Choosing Faith and Morality

7. **A Brief Story of the Christian Church:**
   A Survey of the Church

8. **The Heart of Methodism:**
   Building a Covenant Community

EDITED BY THE AUTHOR

1. **Foundational Documents:**
   Basic Methodist Documents

2. **Instructions for Children:**
   by John Wesley

3. **Speaking Iban:**
   by Burr Baughman

4. **The Essentials of Methodism:**
   Essential Methodist Beliefs

15986116R00079

Printed in Great Britain
by Amazon